Langdon Elwyn Mitchell

**Love in the Backwoods**

Two Mormons from Muddlety

Langdon Elwyn Mitchell

**Love in the Backwoods**
*Two Mormons from Muddlety*

ISBN/EAN: 9783337297657

Printed in Europe, USA, Canada, Australia, Japan

Cover: Foto ©Thomas Meinert / pixelio.de

More available books at **www.hansebooks.com**

# LOVE IN THE BACKWOODS

TWO MORMONS FROM MUDDLETY

ALFRED'S WIFE

BY

LANGDON ELWYN MITCHELL

ILLUSTRATED

BY GILBERT GAUL

NEW YORK

HARPER & BROTHERS PUBLISHERS

1897

TO

GEORGE RHYFEDD FOULKE

## NOTE

The first story included in this volume, "Two Mormons from Muddlety," was published in *Harper's Magazine*. The story following, "Alfred's Wife," originally appeared in the *Century*, under the title "Lucinda," and is now published through the courtesy of the publishers of that periodical.

# CONTENTS

# ILLUSTRATIONS

# TWO MORMONS FROM MUDDLETY

FOR a fortnight the cold down the valley of the Big Thunder, and, indeed, throughout the forests of West Virginia, had been severe. The Big Thunder froze even at Barr's Crossing, where the current at its lowest was rapid and powerful.

Barr's house—it was a log-cabin of one room—stood facing down stream, just above the point where the little Buffalo Branch slipped into the larger river. Behind Barr's cabin there lay a wide meadow. The mountains hemmed river and meadow in, rising steeply on all sides, covered with forest — hemlock below and hard-wood above. Through this mountain gorge, past the meadow and cabin, the Big Thunder poured its swift stream. During such time as the river was open, Nicholas Barr was ferryman. But every morning for the past ten Nicholas had measured the thickness of the ice at the centre of his "crossing," and at length he was satisfied that the ferryman would not be needed for a month, and, if the cold endured, for perhaps longer.

The following morning, having thrown water on the fire and nailed his cabin door fast from the outside, he and his mule crossed on the ice to the right bank of the stream, and made up the steep road towards Carr's Mill, seven miles away. The week before, he had driven his cows, a team of horses, and a yoke of oxen up to his brother Reuben's, and having made such other preparations as were needful, he could now leave the meadow and the little group of log-buildings to the wild-cats and foxes.

Nicholas Barr was in his thirties, a large man, shaggy-headed and bushy-browed, with a reddish-brown skin, a thick brown beard, and a look of slow and serious good-will. When he had first married he had gone

clean-shaven, and held himself erect, despite his heavy shoulders. After eighteen
months of married life with a woman some
ten years his senior he began to stoop
slightly, and he acquired a new look — a
look of dogged perseverance. The wife
had been of a fretful, uneasy disposition,
taking life hard, but an excellent cook
and worker; and this was a main matter,
for her husband was the clumsiest creature
in the world where victuals were concerned ;
he could scarcely bake his own bread when
forced to do so by some temporary absence
of his wife, and though a powerful man and
used to hardship, he was cursed with an in-
constant and feeble digestion. After three
years of childless married life the wife had
died. Barr straightway began to suffer —
from grief a little, and mightily from the loss
of so excellent a cook. He cried once or
twice for the wife whom he had lost, and
forgetting that he had ever suffered from
anything like ill-temper on her part, was

moved to a degree of sincere sorrow.  But, sitting upright in his bed in the night, he was far more moved by the attacks of heart-burn and indigestion, which, as his own cook, he began now to bring upon himself.

It took him but a short while to have it borne in upon him that he must get a cook. He accordingly came to an understanding with a boy, who was to help him in the farm-work, as well as prepare both their meals.  Two years passed over this arrange-ment.  When on this day of the second winter Barr saw that the river had frozen solidly, he told the boy he might go home and see his people; he wouldn't need him again.

As Nicholas arrived at Carr's Mill, Amri Carr, the miller, came out on the stone steps. Amri was large and ruddy, with a twinkle in his eye.  He looked well fed and fortunate. The dust of the flour whitened him from head to foot.  Even his eyelashes were white. He greeted Nicholas heartily, blowing the flour from his beard, and speaking as if Nicholas were some thirty feet farther away than he was.

"Aren't had no Mormons down the Big Thunder?"

Nicholas said he had seen none such.

"Well," said Amri, dusting his sleeve, "you will; there's two of 'em perusin' these parts —prowlin' round to pervert women folk to be Saints. Tell ye, Nic, these two Mormon elders—youngest elders ye ever saw—they've been a-carryin' on up at Muddlety like time and a jack-knife. Yes, sir! Where are ye p'intin' to?" Amri took a sack of flour by the neck and threw it over his shoulder.

"P'intin' to Rich Valley," replied Nicholas, looking down at his stirrup with some appearance of embarrassment. Amri let the bag of flour drop with a thump, and appeared to prepare himself for a shock. "Just reckoned I'd ride across and see if—she looks as she did—that day. If she looks about the same—why—"

"You won't?" said the miller.

"Reckoned I just would," replied Nicholas.

Amri drew a long breath, stuck his hands in his pockets, and squared himself.

"Why, she was a little green stick of a gal when you saw her! Little winch, little rod of a thing. Hell-to-find, Nic, time flies; sun's been a-shinin' since then. Come summer, come fruit; she'll be all — well, so to say, all bust out into a woman by this!"

"Ride over with me," said Nicholas, irrelevantly to the effect of the sun's shining on the little rod of a thing. Amri replied that nothing would suit him better. Nicholas should stay with him overnight, and the two of them would set out in the morning.

When Amri's family of eleven were packed off to sleep, and while he was preparing his traps for the early start, Nicholas gave him a fuller account of his feelings than he had as yet done.

"'JUST RECKONED I'D RIDE ACROSS AND SEE'"

No, he had not seen or heard of "her" since the evening four years before when she and her father, old Sammy, had come to the Crossing with Amri. But he had always remembered the little girl's face. At first he had wished he had a daughter like that; but, as Amri said, she was a grown-up girl now, and as far as asking her to become his wife was concerned, no doubt when he saw her again he *would* feel differently; but at all events he was going to see her.

Amri had seen her the winter before, and he affirmed now that his cousin D'liss was just as pink and white and pretty as a plumtree blossom, and that her father old Sammy, he'd taught her to fish and swim, and she could do most anything that was no use to do. "Yes, sir, and she's about as useful round the house as a tame coon or a catamount, providin' his will was good."

To this Nicholas made no answer. He remembered a face in the twilight on the

raft crossing the Big Thunder.  He was going
to see that face again.

Three days of hard riding through a snow-
storm brought the two men to Rich Valley.
The valley was thickly settled, and was
tapped at the southern end by a railroad.
"Old Sammy," a little man with a red face
and yellow hair streaked with gray, greeted
his cousin Amri with warmth, and said, abruptly, that he liked his friend's look.  His
four daughters — with a wave of his hand
towards the farm-house — would be glad to
make them welcome.  But when he heard
the quest upon which Cousin Amri's friend
had come, he said frankly that he didn't
think his chances amounted to those of a
gone coon ; but, dang him, he might try !
If D'liss chose to live in a log-cabin, why,
dang her, let her do it !  Did he know
D'liss?  Well, D'liss *looked* frail, but whip-
cord wasn't in it !  D'liss was quiet, but
she was better company, begol, than a dog
or a gun !  And D'liss was a gal o' spirit ;

and if D'liss couldn't bow her fiddle, well, then, he, old Sammy, hadn't ever been thirsty in his danged life ; and D'liss, though she had a pinky color, and though she was slim as a young hickory—well, never mind, it didn't make any difference to old Sammy,—but if she didn't have an arm and a will like a rib o' steel—oh, geepheu !"

After this statement they had drinks all round, as if to prepare Nicholas for the will, the strength of which was connoted by the power and oddity of the oath employed.

In the evening they sat about the stove in the parlor. As Nicholas looked about the room and saw the rich crimson and pink wall - paper, the six chromos, the luxurious carpet, the chairs, and above all the red-hot stove, he began to have visions of his own log-cabin. He could hear the Big Thunder roaring coldly; faint, exasperated tones of his first wife's voice became audible to his inner ear. How cheerless the gorge and the gray woods must look ! Nicholas's eye dwelt meditatively on the red sofa. There was no sofa at Barr's Crossing.

Suddenly he gave up all hope. His heart sank; he concluded he was on a fool's errand, and at the same moment the door opened, and Sammy's youngest daughter entered.

She was slim and frail-looking, with soft yellow hair, long, narrow eyes, and a bright color. There was a dreamy expression upon her face that might have gone with a drooping figure; but she held herself erect, and apparently suffered from no hesitations or embarrassment. Nicholas knew her at once. That was how she had looked years ago— even to the wisp of hair which strayed down one cheek. He determined he would try his luck.

Delia Delissa May, as her mother, Mrs. Sammy Cartright, had called her, after the heroines of three novels, read opportunely before the birth of this her last baby, was, above all else in the world, her father's

"TO PREPARE NICHOLAS"

friend.  This filial amity had been at first
based on the fact that she never talked
when he was fishing.  In time she learned
to fish herself, and became therewith his
chosen and constant companion.  She was
tireless, and enjoyed the open air.  Moreover, when her father had drunk as much
as Delissa from long and necessary obser-
vation thought was wise, she made a habit
of stealing his flask out of the coat which
generally lay on the bank and of hiding it.
Old Sammy, on discovery of the theft, always acted as if it had never happened before.  He swore roundly; accused Delissa;
called her a thief; to which she responded
on each new occasion with a set form of
words: That she had not seen the bottle,
and she hated the sight of it, and she wished it was dead.  Old Sammy made a point
of accepting this statement without demur;
and the fishing, with no drinks between fish,
went on as before.

The girl's mother had died while she was

still a child. Her elder sisters had thus
grown into the habit of taking care of the
house, marketing, sewing, and the like; and
Delissa accordingly had time to fish, to read
novels and adventures, to play her violin, to
comb her yellow hair before a little looking-
glass in her own room, and occasionally to
be rather more flattering in her manner to
some young farmer of the neighborhood
than her lack of special interest in him war-
ranted.

It happened that her grandmother, who
survived the mother, had made the trip
across the Alleghanies in a wagon while yet
she was a girl. She often related to her
grandchild the many pleasures and hard-
ships of the journey. The child's picture
of the old woman's story, with the lives of
Dave Crockett and Daniel Boone, and yet
other accounts of more obscure heroes of
the woods, had entered into her mind deeply. Her father's manner of bringing her up
contributed to foster this influence, as did

certain traditions of the family; for her
father's grandfather had fought a pitched
battle with the Indian chief Shaweengo in
the old days in Kentucky. And even now
there was an uncle who had sold his wretched house and farm in "old" Virginia, and was
prospering, deep in the woods and mountains behind the Alleghany Ridge, and who
every fall wrote to her father to come out
and kill deer, and go bee-hunting with him.
It was to this uncle's log-cabin she had been
taken four years before. She remember it
as the most wonderful place in the world.
There was a tame bear cub there, and the
men were very gentle and respectful to little
girls. Since her earliest childhood she had
always cast her eyes longingly, therefore,
towards the sun as it set over the unbroken
forest, and felt in her little heart that there,
where the sun seemed to hasten in his going down, there lay a world of wonder,
of romance, danger, hardship, and pleasure
—all very different from the life of Rich

Valley, with its railroads, hotel, and corner
grocery.

She was therefore not a little pleased
when she heard that Nicholas had ridden
across the mountains and through the winter
snows to "see her face." She remembered
him only as a bearded giant, who had poled
her across a dusky, great river in the winter-
time; but when she understood that he had
buried his first wife she drew back, and told
her father that the sooner his friend went
home the better for all concerned.

Nicholas was sorely put to it how to win
the girl, and this saved him; for he ended by
making no effort whatsoever. But his astonishing skill with an axe and his very considerable strength made an effect, as did his
easy good-humor. The girl was piqued
also that he was not more jealous of her.
For he appeared to be rather kindly disposed
towards her other admirers; and after a
month or more she began to hate him.
This hate caused her many sleepless nights;

and it was not long before she looked pale,
and presently the day came when she seemed to herself to have lost her pleasure
in fishing.   They were married a week
after this.   Nicholas had intended to have
stayed yet another week with old Sammy;
but the spring thaw had set in, and he began to hear the Big Thunder in his dreams,
and men hallooing vainly on the opposite
bank.

They started therefore the third morning
after the wedding.   The two mules stood
saddled in front of the house in the early
twilight.   Her sisters wished Delissa every
sort of happiness, and gave her keepsakes
without number.   Her father told Nicholas
to be good to his little girl; he kissed her,
and told her to be a good woman, and to
think o' him; and God dang him if he'd ever
go fishin' again as long as he lived.   Delissa
gave a happy sob or two as she rode off into
the morning twilight with her husband.
Old Sammy retired to the wood-shed, sat

down on the chopping-block, and cried like
a child for five minutes.

On the evening of the fourth day Delissa found herself on the sandy shore of Big
Thunder, and presently she was sitting before a sparkling fire in her husband's cabin.
She was cold, tired, and hungry; but she was
moving in a strange dream of happiness.
The rough-hewn logs of the cabin, the pegs
with Nicholas's fishing-rod and powder-horn
and rifle, the strings of onions and beans
which appeared through the cross-slabs of
the loft, the buck-horns and bear-hides, the
immense chimney-place, and the unceasing
roar of the waters outside—all this was just
as she had foreseen it. When Nicholas bore
a heavy log in for the fire, she remembered
the picture at page 110 in her *Life of Daniel Boone*. She wondered if the hero was as
large as her husband.

Nicholas thought that they had best cook
them some supper. The two went out to
the " kitchen," which was merely a second

log-cabin of the same size and shape, standing about a rod from the " house," as Nicholas called the first one.    Here Delissa again
watched her husband light the fire, and lost
herself in her new happiness.

" Now, then," said Nicholas.

" Now, then," repeated Delissa, softly.

" I'll get the stuff out o' the saddle-bags,"
said he, "and then you might cook us supper."

" Who ? — I ?" cried the girl.    " Why, of
course I will, Nic ; only I'm afraid I can't !"

" Can't cook, D'liss?" said her husband.
" Why not?"

" Why, yes, I *can*—if you'll teach me," she
returned.

Nicholas cooked their supper, and at the
same time showed his wife how it was done.
She listened to him, and said " Yes, yes,"
very intelligently, while all the time she kept
wondering if Daniel Boone could have been
as powerful a man as Nicholas.

Her husband, for his part, thought he had

never heard anything as sweet as her laugh
of happiness as she hung her fiddle on a
peg beside his long rifle, and placed the
small looking-glass she had brought beside
that.  When she turned he was looking at
her with an odd expression.

"Why, Nic, what's wrong?"

"I b'lieve I never did know just how
lonesome I was all those years!"

Delissa was about to throw her arms
round his neck when the door, which had
been on the crack, was pushed open, and a
gaunt, lean, bedraggled yellow cat entered
with such a yowl as might have meant
either joy or despair.  Delissa gave rather a
start, and Nicholas looked concerned.

"That's that cat!" said he.  "He's had to
forage for himself since I went courtin' you;
'pears like he hadn't done himself no great
credit."

His ribs could be counted with certainty.
Delissa stooped down and stroked the puss.
Puss purred.

"What's his name, Nic?"

"Well," said her husband, twining his fingers in his beard and looking somewhat embarrassed, "I called him Old Rusty, but *she* called him—"

"Oh, yes," said Delissa, realizing that this was the wreck of the first Mrs. Barr's cat. "Poor, poor puss!"

Stroking the cat, she wondered vaguely if the first Mrs. Barr had perhaps had a yellow complexion and green eyes. And what in the world should they call him now?

"He's a perfect Misery," said Nicholas.

Delissa laughed. "We'll call him Misery," she said; and Misery, who was ready to respond to any title so it called him to food, had then and there his first honest meal for many a week.

The next morning Delissa ran joyfully down to the sandy beach, and looking back saw her new surroundings by daylight: the two log-cabins; some distance apart from these, and up the river-bank, the log-stable;

and beyond, a dozen bee-gums, a long, low
shed, and a scattering orchard of apple, pear,
and plum trees. The meadow, which was
all of the farm, widened from the point of
sand where she stood as a triangle from its
apex; the remote, irregular base of which
was a line of hills covered with a growth of
sapling and laurel, and at no great distance
rising into a mountain ridge.

It was gray and cold, for the sun had not
yet risen, but the girl's heart was beating
with excitement and pleasure. It was so
unlike Rich Valley!—it was the real backwoods. And what a tremendous, swift, hur-
rying river! And there was the great raft
upon which they had come over. The long
boat was a dug-out; the little fat one must
be the boat Nic had always called the
"tub."

And now the girl discovered the little
rocky island which her husband had once
described to her. It lay more than a hundred paces from the slip of sand where she

stood, and in swift mid-current of the Big Thunder. It was covered with a thickety growth, except for a broad face of rock at the near end. Delissa watched how the lumbering ice-blocks, of which the river was now full, bore heavily down against this rocky surface, and then, divided by it, swept round upon either side, and, beginning to receive the undulatory motion of the rapid, danced heavily, and finally disappeared in the whiteness and roughness of the foaming water below. She thought she would like to sit upon this island. From it she would be able to see the two cabins, the wide meadow, and Nicholas at work. No doubt they would both sit there and fish.

The sun must have risen, for the hemlocks high above her on the mountain-side were a brilliant, clear green in the early light. Delissa stretched her long arms upward, and stood a moment, smiling at the blue sky.

"Oh, oh," she cried, softly, "I'm so happy! I'm just crazy to go fishing!"

" Breakfast, Liss," cried Nicholas from the cabin-door.

" I certainly ought to have cooked it !" thought the girl.

The days passed rapidly and smoothly.

The life, it is true, was rough ; there was not a convenience of any sort; but it was free, it was new, it was in the open air, and it was what she had dreamed.

Nicholas taught her all the art of cooking he knew. After a week's tuition he thought she must have learned a good deal, and perhaps she had better commence to cook for the two. Pretty soon he would have a job of timbering on the Oak Ridge, across the river. It would take him a fortnight, and after that he would have the timber to haul to the mill. Delissa therefore took the cooking into her own hands. She worked early and late at it, and hoped for improvement. She was not sensible of any. She lost, however, several pounds of weight, for it was impossible to escape from the heat of the open fire.

But she persevered. Nicholas devoured whatever was placed before him. It cost him sometimes an effort. But he felt that he owed as much to his wife. If she tried her best to cook for him, he must certainly try his best to eat what she prepared. Without, however, becoming aware of it, he gradually ate less and less; and this left him hungry, at the same time that several severe attacks of indigestion unnerved him, and brought him finally to the pass of being physically afraid of his food. This hunger, which began to grow upon him, was mild at first, but presently it became gnawing.

He wished to God his hens would lay!

About the end of their third week, and of the second week of Delissa's cooking, Nicholas took of necessity to surreptitious midnight repasts. He would slip out of bed, and spend an hour in the other cabin cooking, or endeavoring to cook, for himself. On one of these occasions Delissa, happening to awake, and finding herself alone, slipped out

after him ; but as she came round the corner she saw Nicholas, through the window,
cooking and eating.  She skurried back to
bed, with cold feet, and something of an
ache at her heart—an ache that soon changed
itself into a determination to cook a more
palatable meal for him the next day.

But the next day at breakfast she had no
luck at all.  And when in the evening Nicholas came home from his work on the mountain, hungry and tired, the supper was as
bad as possible.  He said nothing, and he
ate all that he could—it was not much.  His
appetite now, burning, or rather, as it seemed
to him, prowling about restlessly within him,
kept him wide awake all night.  Yet he was
afraid to rise and cook himself another midnight meal, for he judged by his wife's
breathing that she was either awake or
sleeping lightly, and he had no mind that
she should guess how empty he was or to
what a pass his sufferings had brought him.

Indeed, it had gone beyond mere emptiness

with him now.   He appeared to himself to
feel hunger not only in his centre, but in all
his extremities.   His hands and feet tossed
about hungrily; his neck was hungry, that
he knew; and he had a sensation of ravin
at the back of his head.

All night long Delissa lay by his side,
wakeful and feeling exhausted from lack of
nourishment, for her cooking found no more
favor in her own eyes than it did in her
husband's.

The next morning Nicholas felt cross, and
could scarcely help showing that he was so.
The breakfast was more eatable than usual;
but unfortunately Delissa had forgotten the
night before to feed the former Mrs. Barr's
cat, who accordingly strolled in as soon as he
smelled the fumes of meat upon the fire.
Rubbing up against Nicholas's chair, he
purred loudly, and, with a kind of chirrup
midway in the purr, rose lightly and seated
himself in the man's lap.   Nicholas was out
of humor, and seizing Misery by his scruff,

shied him somewhat loosely. The animal laid manfully about him in all directions as he whirled sideways, and catching the table-cloth with half a claw, fetched it after him, the meat and batter falling with the cloth.

Both lay in the ashes. Nicholas for a moment thought he would slay the cat. Instead of doing so, he jumped up, and hurriedly left the cabin. With half an explanation to his wife outside, he rowed himself across the river.

When the girl, running in, saw her own breakfast as well as her husband's in the ashes, and Misery thievishly slinking round the corner, it was almost more than she could bear. She determined that the next morning her husband should take her up to his "law-sister's," Mrs. Reuben Barr. Mrs. Reuben lived with her husband and five young ones just off the road to Carr's Mill. She had promised to come down and help get Delissa settled when first the latter had come to the Crossing. But her husband,

Reuben, was still away, at work in the lumber camps, and till he returned she couldn't leave the children. For, as she said to Nicholas, "to leave the chaps with their eldest brother"—this was General Floyd Barr—"was the same as to give them into the charge of a wild-cat, and a mighty keerless wild-cat at that!"

But Delissa, in view of the mistakes she made, thought that if she could merely see Mrs. Reuben it might be a help to her. She could at least learn from one such visit to bake bread.

As for Nicholas, he felt as he crossed the Big Thunder breakfastless that his hunger had ceased to be a joke. Come what might, he must be fed. He made therefore for his brother's house, and, arriving there, said casually that he'd come to stay the day out. He would not give the true reason for his coming; that would be to prove disloyal to his wife.

As towards noon they sat down at the

table, Mrs. Reuben asked him if he had
heard of the two Mormon preachers who
were up in Muddlety? And had he heard
that Dolly Stout was down with a fever?
"Yes, sir, and that man" — "that man"
was Mrs. Reuben's phrase for one not a
husband — "that man was away, and the
woman there, sick to death, with her two
weaklin' brats."

Nicholas said he had heard that Thompson was away, but not that Miss Stout was
down with fever.

"Not a God's soul o' goodness in the
place!" cried Mrs. Reuben. "She'll die for
want o' wood or food, or both ; and surely I
wouldn't want the worst minx alive to
starve like that!"

Mrs. Reuben, a rosy, fat little body, spoke
roughly, but from a heart which was large
and maternal ; and when she had concluded
her statements, looked with round, wide-open
eyes steadily at her brother-in-law, as much
as to say, "Now, then, do your part."

Nicholas said he would go down and see
to her wants.  He did so later in the day.
Although the worst was over, the woman
was miserably ill; but she could scrape along
if Mrs. Reuben would come for an hour every
morning, and if she could get her next
month's firewood sawed and hauled.  Nicholas felt sorry for her, and at the same time
it occurred to him that the performance of
this duty to the sick woman would enable
him to get his dinner every day for a week
or more at his brother's, and afford at the
same time an excellent excuse to Mrs.
Reuben for his so doing.  He told Miss
Stout to count on him for the wood.

For several mornings after this Nicholas
spent an hour or two splitting and sawing
firewood for Dolly Stout, and doing other
small, needful chores about her rickety, foul
cabin.  And each day he got his dinner at
his brother's.  As Dolly and the dinner were
all one thing in his mind, he said nothing
about her to his wife, pretending always to

take a cold snack or lunch with him to his work.

But in a few days Dolly was up and about and needed no more help, and Nicholas, when he arrived as usual one morning, saw to his surprise a black, fat little figure of a man sitting on the wood-pile reading a dirty newspaper. He liked Dolly little enough as it was, and taking a good look at the new-comer, and noticing especially a pair of white hands, he took the blaze to his brother's without more ado.

Nicholas's timbering on the mountain was now finished, but the road was not yet in condition to haul over. This left him all day at home, and if he was still to get his noonday meal at his brother's he would have to invent and give to Delissa a new reason for being away from her a large part of each day. He told her that he thought he would fish some. He explained with some diffi-culty that the best fishing lay down the river, and that by noon he would be too far away to return to the cabin for dinner. Accordingly he started off every forenoon in the tub. He did, in fact, fish for an hour or more, after which he would stride off through the forest to Mrs. Reuben's, where a hot dinner awaited him, thinking as he went that perhaps now in a few days his wife would have learned how to cook, and thereafter he could abide at home.

Delissa begged him more than once to take her to Mrs. Reuben's, and Nicholas said yes, she ought to go there some day ; but he put the day off, and generally with the same phrase: "He would take her there to-morrow, after breakfast, if it was clear." His wife had never known any one so procrastinative. She was puzzled. Perhaps he had some reason for not taking her to Mrs. Reuben's. In the meantime Mrs. Reuben had come to wonder at the regularity of her "law-brother's" visits. General Floyd had his suspicions, too. And Nicholas found it more and more difficult with

3

each ensuing day to satisfy Delissa on the one hand and his sister-in-law on the other. Being naturally a speaker of the plain truth, he became feebly evasive to his wife, and the more so when she inquired of him : Why was he obliged to fish every day? and why not take her? and why did he never catch anything worth mentioning? and why did he spend such a long time catching the little he did? What happy days she had spent fishing with her dear old Sammy! Delissa would have given the world to have gone fishing with him. She was hurt that he didn't seem to want her. It was now not at all the life she had expected to lead. She even began to wonder if he did possibly get his mid-day meal somewhere else. How else account for his loss of appetite? Perhaps if she gave him a better supper—at all events, she would try.

About noon of a warmish day, General Floyd Barr appeared on the far bank of the Big Thunder. Delissa had no trouble in

" ACCORDINGLY HE STARTED OFF EVERY FORENOON IN THE TUB "

playing ferryman when her husband was away. She had learned how to pole from old Sammy. She brought the raft over to the bank with a swing. As she looked up she saw a shock-headed, sandy-haired, freckle-faced boy, with a pair of keen gray eyes, warts on his hands, and square knee-patches on his breeches.

"How d'ye?" said the General. "Thought you were goin' to drown yourself! My name's Barr. You must be awful tough!"

The General eyed Delissa all over approvingly.

"I guess you could wrastle me," he said. Then, after a moment or two of serious meditation, and while the girl, now on the return trip, was still struggling with the force of the mid-current:

"If I ever have to marry, I'll pick out a woman like you!"

As they landed, General Floyd said he'd come to go fishing with Nic.

"Heard the news?"

Delissa said she hadn't.

" The Mormonizers is come!  Hoo!"

The advent of the Mormons appeared to fill General Floyd with some savage longing, for he seized a stool and brandished it at Misery, who, having kept his eye on the General from the moment he had entered the cabin, now scrabbled out the door and sought safety on the roof.

" Yes, sir," said the General, "they say they just eat young gals!  They're puttin' up with Dolly Stout now."

" Who's she?" said Delissa.

" Why, she's Red Dolly — Thompson's wife, or somethin' like it."

" Who's Thompson?" asked Delissa.

" Why, Thompson's just Thompson." replied the boy, cracking his knuckles with an expression of martyrdom endured in a good cause. " He lives beyond us. Nic, he's been there every day for a week. Guess he told ye 'bout Thompson's Red Dolly?"

" So Dolly is Thompson's wife," said Delissa, busying herself with the fire.

" I don't know; she's young, and she's
good-lookin', and she cooks for him, and
they fight — ought to be his wife, if she
isn't."

"And where's Thompson these times?"
said Delissa.

"Oh, he's away—somewhere," replied the
General, the subject not holding him; " and
these two Mormonizers, they're a-Mormon-
izin' along with her!"

When Nicholas found that he had the
General for a companion on his morning's
fishing, he told Delissa that he would be
back by noon for dinner.

Delissa, as later on in the morning she
set about preparing the meal, felt that a
great unhappiness had fallen upon her. Of
course, there was nothing between Nic and
this Red Dolly. But if he had been there
every day, he had surely gotten his dinner

there—cooked, and no doubt well cooked,
by Red Dolly.  It was for Red Dolly, then,
or for her cooking, that Nicholas had left
Delissa alone for whole days.  No, there
was nothing between them.  But why hadn't
he spoken out?—why hadn't he said, " I
can't eat your victuals !" . . . " Dolly!—Red
Dolly !" and "Thompson's wife, or something like it."  Delissa began to sob, trembling as she walked across the room, carrying the kettle with both hands.  "Oh, it
was bitter !—it was not nice of Nic ;—it was
just devilish of Nic !—oh !"

At the same moment Misery slipped silently in at the door.  The girl, moving rapidly across the room, was beginning to cry,
and, the tears filling her eyes, she saw hazily,
and before she could set the kettle on the
fire, trod heavily on Misery's soft stomach,
who at the moment was rolling about on
his back on the floor in a kind of agony
or delirium of pleasure.  Misery responded
with a yell and a struggle for freedom.  The

girl staggered, upset, and fell almost in the
fire; and the kettle, flying from her, struck
the stone hearth and spilled its contents in
the ashes.  As Nicholas, coming home to dinner, entered the cabin from without, the cat
disappeared between his legs.  Nicholas was
none too early; the girl's skirt had flirted
into the ashes and was aflame.  Dragging
her to her feet, he tore the dress from her
body, and swung her into the middle of the
cabin, and clear of the fire.  The burning
dress he kicked into the fireplace.

Delissa, her face crimson, her eyes full of
tears, her yellow hair tumbled down, stood
before him in her short red petticoat, much
less startled and in fear than still sorrowful
and angry.

One hand having been slightly scalded
and then plunged into the hot ashes, she
held it out, not because it was covered with
ashes, but because it hurt her.

"In the good Lord's name!" cried Nicholas, looking at her, "How'd ye do it, D'liss?"

Delissa made at first no reply. She looked at the fire, and at the contents of the
kettle now mingling with the ashes; and
then at Nicholas himself. Finally she said,
in a trembling voice:

"Misery!"

"I'll slay that cat," said Nicholas, express-
ing that determination for the hundredth
time.

Delissa looked again at the fireplace, in
which the dress was flaming brightly, again
at Nicholas, who was looking at her, and last
surveyed herself: her short red petticoat
and gray stockings, and her wounded hand
held out to one side. Her face began to
twitch with sympathy for the poor girl whom
she saw in this horrible plight. She suddenly burst into tears.

"I knew it would come to this," she
sobbed.

Nicholas for the life of him couldn't tell
why, but he began to feel guilty.

"I don't know what you brought me here

for! I could do well enough if it wasn't for—her cat. Nothing I can do suits you, or him. He—he's a wicked devil, and he knows it! I'm heartsick of it all. And where you spend your time nobody knows, nor I don't know if you know yourself; when you fish even you catch nothing!"

The child spoke the words in a gentle, low voice and brokenly, for she was sobbing. The tears streamed down her cheeks, although her face was uncontracted; only her lips quivering and her breath coming irregularly.

"Maybe you're tired of me; or you think I might learn quicker how to — c-cook. I should ha' thought if a man loved a girl he would put up with—with—'most anything," —through Delissa's mind passed visions of all the unmistakably palatable dishes she had prepared; Nicholas thought of the hungers he had endured;— "rather than to go philandering off up there with a Red Dolly woman. I've had lovers too; I'm not so poor but I can have 'em yet, if I've a mind to."

Delissa's eyes lightened through her tears, and she gave her head a little toss. But the threat was made in a voice and tone which would have perfectly carried the words, " I love you still, and you might say you're sorry."

Nicholas hesitated, feeling dumb and confused. The girl wanted him to come to her, so she moved a step back, her heel as she did so striking the tall wooden cupboard. The china ranged along the shelves rattled ominously; and the big tin dish-pan, filled with boiling water to be ready for the cleaning up after dinner, shook and splashed. " Don't—don't," said Nicholas, seeing her elbow approaching the dish-pan.

But Delissa had derived a certain confidence from the thought of her former admirers. Her voice took a clearer tone, and she pushed the dish-pan farther back on the shelf on the cupboard with her elbow, with-

out looking round.   This brought the pan
too near the corner.    Nicholas motioned to
her to take care.

"I don't care for anything, now," said she,
with as much defiance in her manner as her
natural gentleness and the sweetness of her
voice would admit of.   "No, sir; I don't!"
with a flirt of her body and another light
toss of her yellow head; and, her burned
hand hurting her suddenly, she held it out
in the must pitiable manner, as she continued: "Things must change.   If you want
to go and live with Red Dollies—"

"Live with Dollies!" exclaimed Nicholas.

"I hope she cooks all right."

"Cooks all right," said Nicholas, repeating her words in astonishment.

"So you did get your dinner from her?"
cried the girl.

Nicholas was about to say where he had
got his meals when his wife broke in upon
his preparations for speech, which at the best
of times were slow.

"You can cook for yourself after this.  I can catch fish, if I can't cook.  And I hate it, and I've just a mind to give up, and leave off, and quit, and do nothing, never, any more!"

Delissa's eyes began to sparkle, and though she still held the burned hand to one side, she threw the other bravely forward as if to loosen it from the thraldom of her sleeve, a gesture indicative of her new determination to give up, leave off, quit, and do nothing never for evermore!

"It's too much for—for a girl," she continued, looking reproachfully at her husband. "You might ha' tried to eat—you might ha' pretended; it wouldn't ha' hurt me to have encouraged me a little teeny bit.  And you never drowned the cat when you said you would, and you know he thrusts himself between us.  Maybe you like him better than you do me—"

Delissa had become softer again, and, having exhausted all her real pleas, was en-

gaged in manufacturing others against Nicholas, as this of his not drowning the cat, she
having made him solemnly and with a kiss
swear to her only the day before that he
would harm Misery under no circumstances.
She now ended up with saying, as she looked
tearfully down and away from Nicholas:

"Why don't you say something?"

Nicholas held out his hands deprecatingly.
He had things to say, but he had first to
marshal and compose them into a proper
order, and he was tortured with fear of the
china's unsetting above Delissa's head in one
of her erratic movements of despair. So
that finally—partly from real affection and
partly out of a desire to avoid the impending
smash—he said, as the girl stood looking
away from him and drying her tears:

"Come over to me, D'liss—come here!"

The girl caught something in the tone
of his voice that was not altogether what
she wished or expected; it was not loving.
She turned half round from him and burst

into a storm of sobs, repeating again and
again :

"You don't love me now—you don't love
me any more, not any more, never any more,
never! I half believe you d-do care for that
r-red thing! She can c-cook."

Nicholas was distracted. He had never
seen her really cry before. The first Mrs.
Barr's tempests had all been dry, and in the
nature of anger. As he saw the tears wet-
ting Delissa's cheeks and chin, even, and her
blue eyes looking at him reproachfully, he
felt that he could better endure slow death
by fire, and that he loved her Heaven knows
how much. But he was still frightfully anxious about the china, and indeed, before he
was able to do more than say the girl's name
in a pacifying manner, her burned hand, as
she turned to lean against the cupboard,
came between the wood-work and her petticoat, and, paining her smartly, she withdrew
it upward. The dish-pan of hot water was
in the way and tilted with the force of the

blow her elbow gave it. Nicholas rushed
forward, with both hands stretched out, to
save it from falling.

Delissa, supposing he meant the out-
stretched hands for her, drew as suddenly
away, and over went the tin pan, deluging
the floor of the cabin, and, in its course
downward, washing Nicholas's two hands
with water hot enough to burn a little and
to make him suppose that he was burned
badly.

He uttered a growl and wrung his hands.
Delissa, seeing what had happened, stopped
crying in a flash and looked at him aghast
with the fear that he was really burned.

" Burned 'em," said Nicholas, savagely,
and as if to himself.

" No, no," cried the girl, and ran to a shelf
to get a bottle of oil. She brought it to
Nicholas, her face changed suddenly from
self-pity to the tenderest fear and compas-
sion. Nicholas looked at the bottle. It
was really too much for him. He regarded

Delissa with some severity, and then said dryly:

"Vinegar!"

The girl looked innocently at the bottle, which she had uncorked. There was no label; she smelled it; it was vinegar. As she turned hastily to the shelf, Nicholas took up his hat, and with a call to the boy outside to accompany him, strode down to the beach and rowed angrily across the river in the tub.

When Delissa saw that her husband had indeed gone, that she was left alone, it seemed to her as if the very heart of the world had ceased beating. She watched him and the General pull the boat up the beach. They disappeared in the twilight and brushwood.

She shut the door and sat down on a stool. An hour passed, and then another. It was all over now, and no doubt she had been wrong from the beginning. But why in the name of sense had they not taught her to cook? Was there a thing more mysterious than that there was nothing whatever about cooking in the novels? They eat the most abundant and the most savory "viands," but who in Heaven's name cooked the viands?

Davy Crockett and Daniel Boone cooked for themselves—Nicholas couldn't. She had done her best, all to no purpose. And now —Red Dolly! and doubtless Nicholas would go tell *her* all about his "wife"! As for Misery, he was the devil in cat form; he was possessed; or else the first Mrs. Barr was in the cat; at least, the cat sided with the first Mrs. Barr in every hair of his body, else why did he always trip her up? It made no difference; it was all over—cooking, all her efforts, her self-restraint, and—and—love— and Nicholas didn't care for her now—and indeed why talk about it? It was all over! If she could upset herself in the river, if the bottom would unexpectedly fall out of the boat, then she would drown. Nicholas would see her lying at the bottom, all white;

4

or if some brutal man would happen in and
kill her, then Nicholas would find her body
lying right across the threshold. The tears
began to rise.

Three light knocks were given upon the
cabin door. After a moment or two they
were repeated. Delissa had started to her
feet with the first knock, but before she
could make up her mind to bolt the door
the latch clicked. The door opened ; a long,
white, hairy hand appeared, clasping the end
of the door, followed by an arm in seedy
black as the door pushed open wider.

Delissa fell back several paces, the blood
rushing to and fro, from her heart and to
her head, and back again, as she fixed her
eyes on the door, now at a standstill.

" May godly strangers receive welcome
here ?" said a voice, hollow enough to have
been followed by a racking cough.

" Visitors from the Lord," rapped out
another voice, quickly, lightly, and in a tone
that evinced an eager desire to see inside.

Delissa would have spoken if she could. As she gave no reply, the door farther opened, and Delissa saw slowly enter a tall, pale man, followed by a short, fat one. Her breath came quick.

" We are peace-lovers," said the tall man, unctuously.

" Peace-bringers," followed up the little one, at once echoing and outdoing his brother, who blocked both his vision and entrance by standing full in the door-way.

The tall man, whom Delissa now saw to be of a doughy white complexion and bald-headed, cast a pair of large brown eyes upon her inquiringly. As she merely gasped in reply, he came farther in, allowing his younger fellow to enter, which the younger fellow did briskly.

He also looked inquiringly at the girl, but, receiving no answer, both men, having learned the custom of the country through which they had travelled for some months, directed their eyes towards the floor, and sat down in the chairs nearest them. Delissa recovered herself suddenly on seeing them seated, and said,

" You can come in."

Not knowing what to do next, she sat down and folded her hands in her lap. But a side glance of the younger man suddenly apprised her of the fact, of which she had been forgetful, that she was in her red petticoat, and that as this petticoat was short, more was visible than should be. She stood up as if shot out of her seat, and reddened.

What to do? She was afraid to leave the two men for a moment, and her other dress was locked up in a box in the house. She turned abruptly away from the men, whose eyes were still fastened to the floor, and began angrily washing the ashes from her burned hand. A hot sensation all over her body told her that both men were using their opportunity to examine her from top to toe. She became aware also that the kettle could still be seen lying on the stone hearth, and

that the water-pan was upside down on the
floor.   There was a moment when she could
have sat down on the floor herself, in the
thus lengthened and decent midst of her red
petticoat, and told these two wretched Mormon creatures (for she guessed them to be
such) to go about their business.   But her
hand began to smart her, and at the same
time the tall, elder man spoke.

"We are came to ask a night's lodging,
and we are came to spread the great news—
the gospel 'cording to Smith—and—"

The Mormon lengthened out his "ands,"
dwelling on them with a long, twanging
drawl.   This gave him good time to beat up
his next idea, and to bring it out in rounded
form.

Delissa still kept her back to the two men,
mainly out of a sense that if her ankles
could be seen that way, as well as any other,
at least she couldn't see that they were being
seen.   The younger man now interrupted
rapidly :

" Blessed are they 't hold to the prophet ;
blessed are the Latter-Day Saints," he said,
skurrying over the words in a sharp, high,
singsongy voice, and in such a way that
the words seemed pitched out headlong.
" Blessed are the—  You've hurt your hand,
Mrs.—?  Let me—  What?  Yes, certainly."

Delissa flushed a bright pink.  But before
she had half an idea of what was happening,
the little man, with skilful, quick, white, fat
fingers, had lapped her hand about with oiled
rag—oil and rag both produced from his
own pocket—and had carefully tied a piece
of dirty ribbon around the whole.

" There, Mrs.—?"

" Barr," she replied.  " My husband, he'll
be in shortly.  You can stay; he'll see you.
I thank you for—"  She held out her hand
shyly.  " I guess he'll be here soon."

Silence ensued, during which Delissa was
enabled to observe her guests more narrow-
ly.  The tall man had sunk together on his

chair, and was rubbing the knuckles of one hand gently in the palm of the other. Delissa disliked him. He wore a flowing brown beard. This growth, hanging from his sallow face and lank neck, swept abundantly over a time-yellowed shirt-front. But his head was as sterile of hair as his jaw was profuse. What there was grew almost on his neck, hiding his absence of collar with a thin, glossy brown fringe. The absence of hair above seemed to have indecently exposed a pair of enormous ears.

Still continuing to play softly with his hands, the tall man opened and shut his mouth once or twice with a licking sound, and then, in his deep voice, "Ball!" He inclined his head slightly to one side, as if in sorrow for what he was about to say, and looking towards where his younger companion was seated, he repeated, with a caressing inflection, "Ball—Ball's name. Li Ball."

Delissa wondered if she would have to sew up the holes in the little man's elbows.

She guessed not, as his black waistcoat was held together by two safety pins, in place of seven long-departed buttons. He had not shaved for a week or more. She hoped Nicholas wouldn't lend him his razor.

Since the elder man's delivery of the word "Ball," in mournful tone and with deprecative glance, the girl had no doubt that Li Ball was his own name. She thought it might relieve the strain if she ventured further in the same line.

"And your friend, his name?" she said, looking to the tall man for the information.

"Ball's friend's name," put in the little man suddenly and lightly; "I'm his friend," he added, more slowly, and pointed with his thumb to his own bosom. "My name's Ball—Li Ball. His name," he continued, nodding toward the tall man—"his name is Sidon—Dank Sidon."

Delissa realized that they made a point of naming each other, as perhaps being more modest.

" Well," she said, having now recovered herself so far as to have determined to accept the shortness of her petticoat, and to make the best of the Mormons — " well, I expect you're both hungry."

Mr. Ball said with vivacity that he was.

Mr. Sidon made the licking noise that he had before, which signified that he had said, or would like to be considered to have said, precisely what his little friend had.

For a moment Delissa looked helplessly about her.  She made up her mind promptly.

" Mr. Sidon, Mr. Ball, I a'n't no account of a cook; and the fact is I spoiled one dinner to-day already; and I'm afeard you'll have to look elsewhere for victuals, or else wait till my man comes home; and if you get it then I don't know, or any other time in this house unless you cook it yourself," she added, after a pause, and smiling at an idea in itself so absurd.

" Li," said Mr. Sidon, deliberately—" Li, cook."

Li sprang at once to the fire and began to rake among the coals. As Delissa watched him in some surprise, he said : " Saw y' had— course y' did—we all have—trouble. Burned hand, dress — course, too bad ! Lost y'r dinner — too bad ! What ? Yes, certain- ly !"

Mr. Li Ball hurried over the beginnings of his words, spurted out what remained, and chewed off the ends, speaking all the while with a sharp, clicking voice, and glancing furtively about the cabin from under heavy black eyebrows. If unanswered by Delissa, he answered himself by " What ? Yes, certainly."

She wondered how a man could be at once so fat and so quick in his motions.

" You can cook—if you can," said Delissa.

" Can't *you ?*" said Mr. Ball, turning upon her.

Delissa flushed and felt angry. Mr. Ball became aware that something was wrong.

" Can't cook ? Too bad ! What's husband

say? Nothin'? Thinks a heap, guess! What? Yes, certainly! I'll learn y' cookin'. —D——, get a log for th' fire. Certainly will!—Spiled his dinner, eh? Burnt dress, eh? — hand, too — terrible pain! Nothin' easier! Take lessons me! Y' know she brought him butter in lordly dish — there was feastin' in Bible: eat and drank and was merry for to-morrow they died! Why not? Certainly! Too bad! Of course they did! —I'll teach you!"

Delissa showed Mr. Ball where the various needful stores were kept, and while he was bending over the fire slipped out of the kitchen cabin.

When she came back she had on a blue dress. As she entered the door she observed, with a sudden increase of heat, that Mr. Ball's eye slipped down quickly to where her ankles had been previously visible, and as quickly slipped away again in search of some plate or saucer necessary to his operations as cook.

" Dinner's ready," he now said. "D——, dinner."

D——, thus addressed, elongated himself, and sat down willingly enough at the table. He blessed the food with unction, his eyes fixed steadily upon it.

The meal was tolerably silent. Once during the eating Sidon, without premonitory symptoms of any kind, and as if moved by an inward humor, broke into a hoarse, loud guffaw, a kind of cackle.

But immediately, and as if anxious to remove any bad impression this outburst might have caused, he turned to Delissa, and remarked with distinguished irrelevance:

" 'R appetites, Mrs. Barr, are given us to cons'crate."

He helped himself to more molasses, while Ball glanced about in all directions, and busied himself partly with eating and partly with the making of hot cakes.

"What we can't cons'crate we must pluck out.  Pluck it out," continued the Saint, in

a hollow singsong, at the same time extract-
ing a chicken bone from his mouth, with
apparent danger to his hand—"pluck it out
and cast it from you." He cast the chicken
bone into the fire. "A degraded appetite is a
degraded man. A degraded man is—another
biscuit, Brother Li—is a fiend in human
form; and a fiend is a disgrace and a shame
to the place he lives in and the neighborhood
that suffers him; yes, a fiend is a burrnin'
shame!" Sidon burred his "r's" furiously.

Mr. Ball, who thus far had kept the
corners of his red lips turned piously down,
now, with a suddenness that was astonishing, twitched them into a grin that caused
the fat of his face to rise up in lumps in odd
places, and was near to abolishing his eyes
out of his head.

"That's it," he said, evidently restraining
his sense of humor with difficulty—"that's
what a fiend is!—Certainly! Have more
molasses?—He's the wisest man, Mrs. Barr?
Yes, sir! He's a 'possle!—More coffee?—

Too bad about husband! Dare say perfect man! I thought so! Lived long in wedlock? — No! — Happy state! Oh, yes! course! Oh, perfect!"

Ball rose to make cakes.

Sidon, munching heavily, continued, following the food about with his eyes:

"Brother Li is right. Wedlock is the gate through which the saints enter into bliss unspeakable. Oh, can't have too much of a good thing!—Butter, Li."

Mr. Sidon's voice seemed to drip with fatness as he spoke. Delissa was not certain whether he had said that wedlock or butter was a bliss unspeakable.

He continued in more and more of a singsong: "Ah, the grace o' God! That's what we all need here below! We're ugly:—we want grace; — we're in disgrace: we want grace; — we're disgustin', mis'rable, dirrty sinners—liars, and horse-thieves, and beastly bishops of false churches, and forgers of false checks. Do we repent? Nay! We

return to our pleasurable vices as the dog to
his vomit:—see, now, that's where we're not
graceful!—not full of the grace o' God.
Oh, oh, we're at best but human hogs. Hogs
we are born, hogs do we remain, and as hogs,
hoggishly, do we become extinct. Pray for
grace—not to be a human hog! A-n-d"—
Sidon lengthened this "and" out beyond all
the others to signify an oncoming climax—
"a-n-d finally, brethern and sistern, we kin
gyrate and circumlocute, but we're nothin'
but dirrt—dirrt"—he seemed to take a delight in the word—"and damned dirrt at
that, unless the grace of the Church is spread
upon our souls.—Molasses, Li."

Mr. Sidon, who by this time had eaten
enormously, sat back in his chair.

"Husband home soon?" inquired Mr.
Ball, wiping his red lips.

Mrs. Barr thought he would be home soon.

"Eat now? or wait?" continued Ball;
"wait, I guess; good; too bad 'bout burnt
hand!"

"Better than a burrnt soul," said Sidon, with his burr. "Better to marry than burrn!" he added, out of a clear sky.

Ball looked furtively at Sidon, as if he wished he would stop. Sidon continued,

"You're a lonely woman, a-livin' here, Mrs. Barr."

"Oh, my husband, he—"

"Ha'n't you never thought what it might be to see the crystal pavement, the golden towers, the silver houses, of the Great City? Ha'n't you? No; you ha'n't! You're buried; oncet in these woods, twicet in sin! O—h, come out!"

Sidon's voice almost roared.

Ball left the table and took a chair against the wall. His eyes slipped restlessly about. He seemed ill at ease.

"We," continued Sidon—"we are Latter-Day Saints. There were saints in olden times, daughter."

Delissa recoiled within herself from this address, but she showed no sign save to

move to the opposite corner of the cabin
and sit down on a bench.

"But we are the Latter Saints: like the
latter rain, we visit the earth gently." Sidon's voice seemed once more to drop with
fat. "Let no man deceive you, daughter;
we're no friends to sin;—oh, no! We're the
salt of the earth; our savor is not lost;
we're the sweet burnt sacrifice, smelling in
the nosterils; our mouths drop waters of
wisdom; oh, daughter, the tongues of those
whom Smith hath come strongly upon are
steeped in honey."

Delissa began, she knew not why, to feel
hot all over. Mr. Ball was playing a sort
of devil's tattoo with his feet, resting on his
heels, and quivering the toe ends of his
boots at a tremendous rate.

"The playsures of the soul are pu-er,"
shouted Sidon, with uncalled-for vehemence.
"Come out to us!"

Delissa was about to say something to
the effect of her husband's having a voice

in the matter, when the younger Saint
spoke.

"Bring husband out," said he, abruptly,
and kept up the silent tattoo his toes were
playing on the air.

"Bring him," said Sidon, rising and
straightening out the several joints and com-
partments of his frame, until the entire lank-
ness of him was erected to its full height.
Delissa rose too.  She was growing angry,
and at the same time afraid.

Ball's eyes twitched about more rapidly
than ever in his head.

"Oh," continued Sidon, "be gen'rous;
give your husband; give yourself!  Be not
mean like them at Muddlety, that give only
bruises and blows to the Saints.  Oh, there's
a hell that longs to feed on sinners!  There's
a House, and its rafters are fire, and it's
shingled over with slabs o' hot fire, and all
thine enemies shall fry therein, in the fat of
their own mean thoughts—o—h!—"

Sidon's recollection of what he had received from the hands of the Gentiles at Muddlety was lashing him into a frenzy. Ball's tattoo became faster each moment; his fingers, too, were beating on the side of his chair; and his eyes slipped from Sidon to Delissa and back again every instant. Sidon rushed on, extending one hairy hand, and pointing a long finger with a black nail at the end, as if at an object visible to his corporeal eye:

" There, there, over the door o' that House it is written, ' Mene, mene, Tekel!' Daughter, what does that signify? It's an allusion. Where? In the Book. To whom? To Tekel! Nowhere else in the great Book is Tekel mentioned; only there; there he stands, singled out, with that one word pinned to him forever, for all generations to look at. There he stands—Tekel! Mene, mene, Tekel. Not once ' mene,' but twice ' mene.' Tekel, the *meanest* man in the whole world. How mean do you think that man Tekel must ha' been? No meaner than the Gentiles up a-yonder!"

The Saint was rolling voluminously on, borne chiefly upon the sound of his own voice, when the little man twitched his coat-tails from behind, and Sidon sat down quickly, hard, and unexpected to himself. He looked reproachfully at his companion. Delissa, happening to have her back to the two men, was unable to guess the cause of the sudden cessation of Sidon's oratory, but she was thankful that it had stopped. She wished that Nicholas would come back—perhaps now he never would!—if he only would, and throw both the men out of the cabin. As she looked at the hand which the little fat man had so cleverly wrapped about, she could have taken a shovelful of hot wood-ashes and flung it in both their faces; and the picture of herself in this action passed fleetingly before her mental vision. She turned towards the two visitors again. thinking angrily how Sidon's beard would sizzle and smoke with the coals in it; and how, as for the little man, with his heavy black eyebrows and red lips—but before she could imagine the proper torture to be meted out to him, she caught his eye. She colored faintly, feeling that her detestation must be painted upon her face.

But Ball, as for the first time he squarely met the girl's glance, thought simply that she looked very soft and female, and that without doubt they could induce a person of that gentleness and facility of disposition to fall in with their plans and join the "Church."

Delissa, not liking to be inspected so closely, looked again at the younger Saint as if she expected him to say something.

He broke out suddenly: "Since y'r man doesn't come, better go;—h'm,—too bad;—yes; 's late; must go, 'Postle! Just cook you another batch o' hot cakes 'fore I go. H'm!—eh?"

Sidon continued in his unwilling silence, while Ball spent a few minutes in cooking. He covered the hot food carefully with plates

and saucers. When all was done he turned
to Delissa:

"Don't seem to understand cook'ry?—
No; s'pose I come again; give another lesson;—come same hour? Oh, certainly.—
No; no trouble;—you'll learn—same hour to-
morrow. Good-night. Blessed be house!"

The girl had scarcely time to decide
whether or no she would have them come
again, for Ball, seizing Sidon by the arm,
directed him to and pushed him through the
door.

"Oh, the blessing of—"

But Ball had hurtled him out across the
step, and, shutting the door behind them
both, snapped the blessing off short. Sidon's
voice could still be heard outside, rolling
into the darkness.

Delissa felt her heart beat freely again.

As Ball rowed Sidon across the river he
told him he was no small fool not to see the
girl was scared. Now here was their chance.
"That gal was not happy. Her husband

must be cross to her. P'r'aps he threw her in the fire. Certainly; why not? By gol! if he's like that, we'll have her :—she'll come. But tact!"

" Dad burrn it, Ball!" said Sidon, "when religion gets a grip on me—"

" Religion's all well enough in its place; I'm religious at right time."

" It don't grip you," said Sidon.

" Tact, for ev'r'-day use, anyway," replied Ball, tugging at the oars.

" It don't throw you down. 'Pears like it got 'mongst my very bow'ls. 'Pears like I can't holler loud enough. 'Pears like I don't know what I'm a-goin' to say next; but all I've got to do is to open my mouth, and the Lord fills me full o' wor-r-rds! 'Pears like it wasn't my voice I heerd a-speakin'—"

" Voice of a durned fool 's what ye heerd!" said Ball, as he stranded the boat, and with difficulty pulled it up to the spot where he had found it. "I tell ye, tact! There's

verses for it.  Hasn't the Lord foresight?
Well, foresight's where tact commences;
tact is oil on the waters.  Certainly!  The
Lord didn't go and play the fool with Moses;
He didn't command Moses to take up that
serpent by his head, did He?  Nay, but by
the tail.  Certainly.  Well, wasn't that tact?
Dank, ye're lackin' tact!  Just 's tactless as
a sheep."

Sidon, silenced by the example from the
Book, walked wearily up the mountain road.
Ball spent the hour in pointing out to him
that by a little skilful cookery at the right
moment, and a great deal of soft persuasion,
they might win the girl.  They passed the
night at Red Dolly's cabin.

When Nicholas returned, he made no
mention of what had occurred.  But he was
humble, Delissa thought, almost penitent in
demeanor.  When he sat down to his meal
she could have cried.  It was a lie, this
meal!  She would tell him all about the

Mormons. But instantly the thought of Red Dolly crossed her mind. It was her husband's part to speak first. The supper was at all events a well-cooked lie. Nicholas ate heartily. Delissa looked at him shyly now and again, wondering greatly that there was not some trace of Dolly on his countenance; as if "Dolly" must be written there in invisible ink, and perhaps a word would bring it out. Nicholas thought to himself, things are upset, but I won't speak to her to-night; I'll tell her to-morrow after breakfast that I got my dinners that week at my brother's house, and I'll explain about Red Dolly.

The next morning, however, it was rainy, and it seemed to Nicholas far too cold and cloudy to broach such a ticklish subject. After all, D'liss was aware that there were no grounds for jealousy of Red Dolly or of any one else: she knew, of course, that he had been hungry, and had gone elsewhere to be properly fed.

Delissa was therefore left hanging in the
air about Red Dolly, and was by no means
pleased with the position.  But she had not
yet learned to break in upon her husband's
silence.  She determined she would put Red
Dolly out of her mind.  After all, she had
said a great deal too much about it, and no
doubt the General had maligned her.

It continued cold and rainy for several
days.  Nicholas was obliged to set out each
day before noon for Carr's Mill.  He was
hauling the lumber he had cut.  The farm-
work over, he hauled two loads before evening.  He, of course, had breakfast and supper
at his cabin, but instead of stopping at Mrs.
Reuben's for dinner, he took a piece of
something with him in the wagon, and ate
it on the road.  He was determined that,
come what might, he would give his wife no
cause of offence, and would stick to her food
if it cost him his life.

The two Mormons, seeing him pass Mrs.
Reuben's cabin, and inquiring his name,

learned who he was, and his hours of absence from home while teaming it. They took advantage of their knowledge to visit Mrs. Barr at just those hours when her husband was absent.

Their visits were short. Ball cooked supper for himself and Sidon, and, when this was despatched, a second for Delissa and her husband. Delissa asked them nothing for the dinner eaten ; that Ball cooked the second dinner earned, in her opinion, the first.

The Mormons, in order to excite no distrust in Barr's bosom, always avoided the road on which they would have met him with his team, and instead took a " blaze " through the woods to and from the crossing.

The third day of their coming Ball undertook to sound Delissa. This was experimental. He wished to find a weak spot. That there was something wrong in the household he felt sure ; for the very fact that the girl allowed him and Sidon to come each day and cook two meals, and, further,

had very clearly not mentioned the matter
to her husband, was proof enough of this.

First of all, he set about asking her whom
she knew in the neighborhood.  She replied
that she was acquainted with Amri Carr
only, but seeing here a possible opportunity
for gaining knowledge, she asked him if he
happened to know Miss Stout.

Ball heard something perhaps in the tone
of voice which set him on the track.  He
answered by a question: Did she know her?
No? and what sort of a woman was she?
Well—

Suddenly it flashed across his mind that he
had seen Nicholas at Red Dolly's cabin one
morning as he himself had been reading a
paper on the wood-pile.  He conceived it
likely enough that the girl's husband, although he knew Dolly well, had never told
his wife that he knew her; and if Mrs. Barr
hadn't already learned that her husband fre-
quented Dolly's cabin, she certainly would
in the future, and it might be as well to pre-

pare for the time when she did. He proceeded forthwith to paint soot black by
speaking all the evil that he could invent of
Red Dolly. He concluded by saying that
no self-respecting person would be seen near
her cabin; that even so pure and uncontam-
inatable a soul as Dank Sidon's had felt
her abode to be defilement.

Delissa sat spellbound now that she heard
all this from an adult source.

As she thought it over, after the departure
of the Saints, she grew more and more unhappy. The rain was falling in torrents.
Everything had gone wrong that day: she
had broken her comb in the morning, her
looking-glass in the afternoon; four chickens
had died just before dusk; and now as night
fell she heard such news as this.

During the next few days the relation
between herself and her husband, strained
from the moment when she had mentioned
the unfortunate Dolly Stout, grew more and
more distressing and unnatural. He was

silent; he was always silent. Delissa was afraid to speak. She would have given anything on earth to have asked him pointblank about Red Dolly and even to have begged forgiveness for what she had formerly said, and then to have had him clear the whole matter up with a few plain words.

But a silence grew up between them. They seemed to drift steadily further apart.

Nicholas had now enjoyed several days of wonderfully fine cooking. It had surprised him. He was not prepared for the rapidity of the change. Moreover, it was regularly good. The only matter that remained in obscurity was that the cooking at breakfast was invariably poor. However, he did not wish to refer to the matter at all; his wife was progressing, evidently doing her best; and in his slow way he loved her for it—perhaps she was sleepy at breakfast-time. It was odd that she appeared to be so moody, however. · Well, in a few days — as soon as it got warmer — he would speak to her about it.

Delissa, in the meantime, became more sensitive each day to the deceit which this Mormon-cooked meal involved. "I don't tell him a lie," she would say, "but I feed him lies; and I'm a liar!" At another time this would have been too much for her moral digestion, which was properly weak. Now, and as things were, the thought that her husband might leave her forever if she didn't cook well, and the necessity of keeping him away from that horrid, red creature, made the lie seem unavoidable. But her sense of guilty falsehood, of stealthy concealment and subterfuge, combined with the bitter war which her jealousy made upon her faith in Nicholas, deprived her of every shred of happiness and peace.

Her work was a task heavily undertaken and wearily done. And the sleep that followed it was restless and unrefreshing. During this period the girl, her work being over, would pole herself across to the little rocky island, and sit there, feeling dreary and small, amidst the noise of the water.

One such morning, while she sat there, the water of the rapids seemed to make a noise that she had never before heard.   The sky, with that one cloud sailing through it, appeared different to her from any sky she had ever known ;  and the motion of a hemlock bough to and fro as the current caught and released it, caught and released it again, seemed to her strange and sad.   And those two dirty little cabins over there — where had they come from ?   How unhappy it all looked !   How comfortless, and cold, and gray !

She was cold, too.   She saw the warm, yellow light of the declining sun far above the deep, noisy, lonely gorge in which she was.

Oh, if she could live in some place like that, where it was always warm, and golden, and far away !   Yes, she was miserable now.

She must be ugly, too. You were always ugly when you were miserable. But she couldn't see herself any more, since she had broken the looking-glass. She knew her face must look horribly.

There was a small cove in the island, a tiny harbor for leaves and sailing scales of buds, and the like, and almost landlocked by a narrow rib of rock. Delissa went across to it, and, kneeling down, leaned over this pool, supporting herself on her two hands, which she thrust up to the wrists in the shallow water, the pebbles giving way about her fingers.

She looked down into this clear mirror with a deep sigh. The image looked sadly, steadfastly into her eyes—a young girl in a blue dress, pale, and with soft, yellow hair falling forward and about her face. Delissa looked long. Oh yes, she had known it! She *was* ugly now; it was pitiable. Her right hand moving in the water caused ripples to arise, which obscured the image.

6

As face and figure slowly and waveringly reappeared, Delissa sighed again :

"I'm just as miserable as if I'd killed somebody; just as ugly, too.  I hate myself.  You're a liar," she continued, looking at her own reflection, and nodding her head slightly towards it.  "You've very pretty hair —or you had once—but you're just a mean sneak now; and you're jealous—and bad, and—you're just like every wife I ever read of, now—just! and your husband's left you, and he's gone off to some other woman— and you're alone — and it don't make any odds whether you cry or don't!  I've lost my beauty — that's what you have! and all my color; and you're just as ugly and lonely—"

A tear dropped heavily upon the water, and again the image passed fleetly away in ripples, and a shimmering confusion of bright colors took its place.  Delissa began to cry, but still held herself in check till when the image should grow together once more ; but

"OH YES, SHE HAD KNOWN IT! SHE *WAS* UGLY NOW"

no sooner had the light and trembling com-
motion of the waters subsided, and the fair
girlish picture appeared again, than two more
tears, hanging from their lids, dropped together, and shook the living mirror and its
colored shadow into momentary confusion.

Delissa gave a sudden sob, and cried out:
" I haven't even got a glass, not even !—and
I've broken my comb, and he's there now,
somewhere—with her.   Oh, I'm so ugly!
I'm so lonely!"

The tears welled up; she cried bitterly
for relief; even after she had forgotten why
she had begun to cry, she continued, feeling
instinctive need of tears, and of a great many
tears—and these came, accompanied by sobs
which shook her entire body, and to bear
the sudden shocks of which she had to support and brace herself with both hands.

Presently she heard the noise of the water
through her sobs, and through her own mur-
murs of pain, which before she had not
seemed to be aware of, and which still

seemed to call for more sobs to relieve them. But the sobs now came at greater intervals. The water had a comforting, gentle sound. After a while it was over. She felt as if something had happened — something had been broken; a spirit, yearning to be free, was released.

As she sat up it seemed to her that the little brown brambles about her were touching her tenderly. A spray of green brier moved by the breeze swayed against her cheek, and then away again.

The girl lay back, feeling exhausted, against a rock. The rock held her so firmly! The little, rough mosses were damp and cool, as she laid her burning face against them. How kind it all seemed! The air was cool against her eyelids. She surrendered herself to a sense of lassitude, almost of peace. Presently she walked slowly down to the boat, and, bending a moment over the flowing water, bathed her hot forehead with the palm of her hand. It was the most grateful, cold touch. She looked up and saw the fleeting, gray expanse of water. She could almost have thanked the river for its goodness to her.

As she rowed the boat across to the cabin, she thought that perhaps to-morrow might be clear; if it was she would walk by herself to Mrs. Reuben's. The same evening, as Nicholas ferried his yoke of oxen and team of horses across the Big Thunder in a light rain, he saw tracks of men in the mud on his side of the river. This surprised him. He put the team and yoke in the stable, and, returning, examined these traces by the light of his lantern. Two men, clearly. Well, he wouldn't ask Delissa; if she didn't choose to tell him, he supposed it was none of his business. Queer thing, all the same!

The dinner was unusually good that evening. Nicholas remarked it, intending to be pleasant. Delissa flushed. Her husband, looking at her more attentively, thought it odd that, now that everything was at last

going smoothly, good dinners and all that,
she should be still moody and flush.

To - morrow he would certainly tell her
all about where he had got those dinners
—to-morrow as soon as he had hauled his
last load, or at least he would if it didn't
rain.

"You're a-growin' to be a master-cook,
D'liss," he said. "How much flour did ye
mix to the corn meal in that bread?"

Delissa replied promptly that she didn't
know. She appeared suddenly to have
found something that needed her undivided
attention at the far corner of the cabin.
Nicholas thought he would find out who
those men were.

The day following his discovery of the
foot-marks, Nicholas took General Floyd into
his confidence. He thought that as the
General was a boy only going on twelve, he
couldn't have any sense of a family quarrel;
the strained relations of husband and wife

SUSPICIOUS FOOTPRINTS

were all smoke to him; nor would he be able to build a bridge from the effect to the cause; he lacked the knowledge of age and years, and therefore he was safe. Besides, Nicholas, who was the most naturally un-deceitful man in the world, knew that the General possessed a devilish wit and inventive genius in the way of all things indirect and underhand.

He called the boy out of his cabin, where Mrs. Reuben was as busy as usual. The General knew by his uncle's manner that something important was in the wind. He therefore assumed an air of superior listlessness, and came slowly out on the road, snapping his knee-joints as he walked. His jack-knife, with the blade opened, was in his hand. As he advanced towards Nicholas he tossed the knife lightly in the air, and dexterously caught it again, all the while looking at it with an expression which seemed to say: You see, you silly thing, I can always catch you. When he had reached the spot where his uncle stood, he looked at him as if he had just made the discovery that he was standing there.

"Hello, Nic! that you?"

Nicholas said, bluntly and fearlessly, to the boy, who now stood with his hands rammed into his breeches pockets and his eye cocked at his uncle:

"There's men comes about my house—comes in my absence." He looked inquiringly at the General.

"Wife home, Nic?"

"Certainly," replied his uncle.

"D'ye trust her—alone?"

"Why, concern it—"

"Do ye, or don't ye, though?"

"Trust her? What's that—"

"Got this to do with it! If she's sound, means honest, don't ye know, why, what's the odds if a hundred men tramps about her? If she's not sound—'ain't got sense, don't ye know, why—"

"Why what?" said Nicholas, gruffly.

" What's your opinion, anyway ?" said the General, imperturbably.

" Don't know," said Nicholas, glumly, and looking suspiciously at the General.

" Women's women al—ways," said the General, throwing his jack-knife in the air again and catching it. " Say that, don't they ?—the old grandmas ; they had ought to know ; they been women once :—women's women 's what I've heerd 'em say ; guess it means like sayin' a cat's a cat ;—can't trust 'em, not near the cream-pot, sure !"

Nicholas could have cowhided his nephew on the spot. A thousand thoughts, and all of them argus-eyed with suspicions, began to shoot like comets in every direction through his mind.

" What 'n the whole world did I ever ask you to help me for?" said he, at length, angrily helpless of any better answer to the boy's insinuations.

" Ask me to help ye !" exclaimed the General, in his shrillest voice, and elevating his eyebrows so that his scalp moved back on his skull an inch or more, as if his very skin were astounded at such a thing ;—" ask me !—ye didn't ! If ye will, I'll help ye, quick enough."

" Well ?" said Nicholas, savagely.

" ' Well ' ain't askin'," said the boy ; " not fair askin', anyway.  I don't give no hungry man his supper for sayin' ' Well !' "

It was not in vain that Mrs. Reuben had drilled her young savage with elementary politeness.

" Help me, then," said Nicholas.

" Why, I guess it's those two Mormon-izers, Nic," said the boy, sweetly and con-fidentially.

Nicholas didn't know whether it was or was not.  But in any case they must do something.  The General, therefore, having Nicholas now entirely in his grasp, laid a plan of operations.  The next day they were to go fishing together.  They would take their rifles, too.  He, the General,

"WOMEN'S WOMEN, AL-WAYS," SAID THE GENERAL.

would do all the lying that was necessary.
Then they'd turn up at an unexpected moment. As for the Mormonizers, he knew it
was they, because they hadn't eaten a dinner
of Mrs. Reuben's for seven days now ; they
went off every day, and ate, they said, at the
mill ; but they lied in their throats. He'd
seen 'em going in another direction.

The General could scarcely sleep that
night with desire for the coming day. Ever
since his mother had taken up with the two
Mormons, the General had suffered more
than he deemed necessary. He'd be darned
if he could get enough to eat while Old Lick-
chops sat at table! If there was no more
coffee but one cup, Dank Sidon had it ;
if there was one last biscuit, Dank grabbed
it ; if there was a little apple-butter only on
the plate, Dank gobbled it. Dank even paid
visits to the apple-barrel in the corn-crib ;
he guzzled night and day! And, besides,
his hands were wet, and he had two front
teeth wanting. The General could have

roasted him alive on the latter indictment
only.

As for Fatty, he wasn't so bad; he could
play jack-straws (he cheated, though); he
was good enough. But he, the General,
wouldn't trust anybody who moved his hands
about like that. And look at his eyes; he
was *always* looking sideways one way before
he looked sideways the other, just as if he'd
had his hand in your pocket and wondered
whether you guessed it. Both of 'em was
dogs, anyway.

The General accordingly passed a night
made restless by dreams of torture and re-
venge.

Early the next afternoon Nicholas and
the boy set off with their fishing-rods. They
floated past the island, but as soon as the
turn of the river hid them from sight, they
beached the boat and began to fish. In half
an hour Nicholas was on tenter-hooks to go
back. But General Floyd would suffer no
such folly. The Mormonizers must be well

hooked before they drew them in. Nicholas
continued, therefore, to fish savagely, thinking of all things under heaven rather than of
the fish he had caught or was catching, and,
whether or no as a consequence of this absent state of mind, was more plenteously
rewarded with luck than ever in his life before. He drew out dozens of fish.

The two elders came down the mountain
at their accustomed hour. The dug-out was
gone, but the General had taken care that
the "tub" should be on the bank. Ball
rowed his brother clumsily across.

Delissa had suffered from bad dreams the
night previous. These were vague, but
troublous and unhappy. She awoke with a
picture fading rapidly from her sleep-memory
of Mr. Ball very ill disguised in Nicholas's
great-coat, stealing on her from behind, and
whispering that all he wanted was to see if
he could make a nice dish out of her red
petticoat. But no sooner had he begun to
cook it than Misery had upset the frying-

pan, in which the red petticoat was already
no bigger than a little red bean or pea; and
in the dense smoke that followed the over-
turning of the pan suddenly appeared Delissa's wedding-dress — all torn, rumpled, be-
smirched, and in rags. Delissa awoke crying,
and still hearing, "Too bad!" and yet further back in her sleep, a remote cackle from
Sidon, as if from regions of the air.

When, the same afternoon, she saw the
Latter-Day Saints coming across in the
"tub," she made up her mind that it would
be the last day they entered the house.

Ball made unusual despatch in both the
preparing and the eating of his dinner on
this occasion. His eyes shot about from
one object to another, Delissa thought, with
even more than their usual celerity and suspicion. Brother Sidon was silent, save when,
according to habit, he made noises with
his mouth. Once, in a momentary absence
from the cabin, the girl thought she heard
Sidon burst into the first note of his cackle.

She started, for the sound brought the confusion and fear of her dream back to her; but either a fat hand was laid quickly over the mouth of the elder, and the cackle untimely cut off, or else Delissa was nervous and dreaming, this time with her eyes open. When she re-entered, Sidon was drooping on his chair, with the fingers of one hand up the sleeve of the other arm, and on his face a look of settled spirituality.

Delissa wondered how she had ever allowed two such men to enter the house at all.

As Ball finished cooking the second dinner, and the girl had set the table and pushed out of sight those plates which bore the mark of use, Misery was heard miaouing dismally at the door.

Delissa opened the door on a crack and Misery slid through, accompanied by a blast of cold air and the sound of rain.

The girl heard the tall Saint say, in a low voice, to the stout one, "Rain again, Li; better put it off."

There was no audible answer.

The fire had sunk down to a huge mass of glowing wood-coals, which diffused a warm, colored light through the little cabin.

The rafters were red in this glow. The white, knitted socks and dish-rags, hanging on the walls opposite the fireplace, were colored by the same light.

The steel cheek of the axe-head on its pegs and the copper kettle below it cast a red sparkle back to the coals. Misery, who sat as close as in his wisdom he deemed politic to even a dying fire, was, save for the green lustre of his orbs, as red as rust. Even Dank Sidon's long brown beard received a golden polish or gloss from the flame fronting which he sat with his chair tilted against the wall; and Delissa, moving about erect, restlessly, and with her eyes cast down, took from the unseen rays of the fire a warm, golden light over all her person. It lay on her blue dress, on her neck and hands, and made her face, that was pale of late with pain

and anxiety, seem as radiant as it had been
in reality only a few weeks before.

It was the twilight of fire, melting slowly
into darkness as the ashes settled and sank.
Moved by a side glance from Ball, who was
busy wiping the dishes, forks, and knives
which Delissa handed to him after washing,
the tall elder arose.

"The speerit has fallen," he said, adding
suddenly, as he saw Misery rise, hunch his
back, and yawn, "on me! Daughter, will
you join me in prayer?"

Delissa replied that she felt no call to pray
at the moment, but she hoped he would fol-
low his inclination. She refilled the dish-
pan with boiling water, and rattled the knives
and forks about inside so as to make considerable noise. The noise relieved her.

"I will pray," said Sidon, seemingly in a
repentant or depressed condition of mind,
for he began in a very low voice, not to say
melancholy—"I will pray for thee, little
daughter, that thou mayst be like cinna-

7

mon, and aloes, and incense, and nard—oh,
nard—that lend themselves willingly to the
—oh!—Lord's use! That thou mayst be as
sweet, new milk upon the tongue of a
Saint—"

"In Par'dise," snapped out Ball.

Sidon repeated the phrase in his own time
and with his own unction, and began again,
or rather continued, for the volume and flow
of sound which rushed from him were never
wholly silenced, even if the words had ceased
or hung fire:

"May—may—be sensible of the pleasurable touch of the Holy One—"

"As it were!" ejaculated Ball, fiercely, with
a glance at his co-mate. Sidon, perhaps in
irritation, did not repeat the correction, but,
stroking his beard gently, with his eyes a
trifle closed, and slightly swaying to and fro,
he continued;

"And be, and feel, and submit softly to
the fire of the love of the One Body of the
True Church, and that thou, in fine and final-

ly, may be moved, and thrilled, and warmed, and overcome with and by the everlastingly sweet kiss—"

Ball dropped a dish in the pan of water with a splash, and, without turning his head, snapped out, sharply :

"O' th' Lord!—Church's embrace! hm!"

"Of the Lord!" roared Sidon, slowly and deliberately.

"Tact! Tact! Pray for tact, 'postle! Hm!—we need tact, sister."

Ball had now gone so far as to call Delissa by this title. Sidon had come to a grieved and gloomy pause. He now added, in nearly his natural voice, though with his eyes tight shut, that he would pray alone.

"Labor and prayer are not in 'cord," he sighed, with a glance at Ball, who was wiping knives and forks with the rapidity of a machine invented for the purpose. He shuffled softly across the uneven floor, and disappeared in the shed, closing the door after him.

Delissa instantly took fright. The door was shut, and here she was alone with this nasty little weasel—with his fat fingers.

She was afraid now to meet Mr. Ball's eye, and afraid when he glanced sideways at her, as she felt he was at the moment doing, that he would read her fear in her face.

But not even a more acute observer than Ball could have divined the girl's meditations. Her fingers were moving about their work dexterously, rapidly; and she herself, erect and busy, had, if anything, a rather dreamy and inattentive look in her blue eyes.

"W're leavin' t'-morrer mornin'," said he, as he wiped the plate she put down beside him, without lifting his eyes from it.

Delissa made no reply.

"Glad to get shet o' such nuisances, eh?"

Delissa said "Oh no," rather more pleasantly than she would have liked.

"Ain't bent any t'ward our—"

"No," said Delissa, firmly.

"Too bad! Guessed 's much! You're too good—hm! don't need it! yes; no; fact!"

Delissa said that she didn't pretend to be so very good.

"Don't ye?" returned Ball, sharply. Then, sweetening his voice, "Y' have beauty, anyway; beauty's better'n goodness—in a woman—ain't 't so?"

The girl's heart began beating rapidly. But she made no response, and this encouraged the Saint.

"Yes, you've beauty; mustn't blush;— beauty's beauty—gift o' God, eh? Certainly, can't be denied. No, but it's danger— it's danger."

Delissa, fearing to be silent, replied, shakily and at random, that she didn't know much about such things.

The Saint began to tremble down his fat legs. He knew the time had come.

"Yes y' do," he exclaimed, "know all about such things."

Facing her suddenly, he laid one hand on her sleeve. Delissa withdrew the arm.

"Beauty's 'traction; 'traction's pleasure; pleasure's life. Who gives life?—blessed be 's name! Ah, you're beautiful; nobody sees it; ah, nobody has eyes for it; ah, nobody praises it—no, they don't. Y' just waste y'r beauty cookin'; burn it over th' fire; kill it with carryin'; cry it off y'r cheeks all night. Ain't 't so? Know it is! But some sees y'r beauty, some has eyes for it."

Delissa breathed heavily; the blood filled her face; her bosom heaved visibly; her lips parted; she felt a momentary giddiness, and dropped the dish-rag in the hot water, at the same time catching hold of the ears of the dish-pan to support herself. The young Saint's eyes travelled rapidly from the girl's face over her entire length, and back to her face again. He saw her agitation, and interpreted it according to his lights. His hand hesitated in the air, close to her shoulder, without touching it. "There's some sees it,"

he continued, hoarsely. "Some has eyes for
nothin' else in the world; some as 'd perish
ruther n'r see y'r beauty fade out, wash out,
flicker out like a candle, leave y' white, wax—
burnt y'rself out cookin'! Ah! that's it!
Cookin'!"

Inspiration had come upon Sidon in the
outer shed. His voice was now rolling about
to his heart's content, and the floor could be
heard creaking under his pious knees. Delissa had turned her head, and during Ball's
speech was looking out of her soft blue eyes
at the little man, her hands still firmly clasping the dish-pan. Ball rushed on, with barely a pause:

"Y'r beauty;—y' know it—why d' y' hide
it under bushel?—The Lord—I love y'—y'
know it; certainly — you feel it, I see you
do." The Saint wet his red lips, and sweet-
ened his voice again, which he felt had grown
too hoarse. "Course I love y'; look at your
eyes, look at your face; you're a damn fine
wo—good, religious woman; certainly!—and

y're a beauty!—I can see—oh, I can see it.
I love y', and y'r heart says—don't it say?
Certainly does. Amen! Oh, sister—"

Ball was about to throw his arms about
the girl, but something in her face changed
his purpose; he fell on one knee, and, looking up with an impudent smile on his
hot, fat face, encircled her waist with one
arm and laid the hand of the other on her
hip—Sidon bawling meanwhile in the shed
like a calf deprived of its mother's milk.
Delissa, as she felt the Saint touch her,
straightened her slight, wiry frame suddenly,
and with a single lift and swing of the dish-
pan, grasped in both hands, fetched the side
of it against the side of Ball's head, and, tip-
ping it, spilled the contents—hot water, un-
washed plates, knives, and forks — over his
head, face, and shoulders. As the plates
crashed on the floor the little Saint shot back
with a yell, bearing the dish-pan with him
on his head—a gigantic tin hat—which he
instantly and furiously dashed to the floor,

A SAINT'S DISCOMFITURE

and stood wringing his hands, the dirty water dripping and trickling down from his
black hair, chin, ears, and nose, his entire
person, clothed and naked portions alike,
steaming, and his mouth sputtering furiously. The prayers in the shed ceased. Delissa darted to the front door in anger and
fright. There she remained, facing Ball, her
hand on the latch, fearing both to leave the
cabin and to stay in it. Ball began to curse
between his howls of rage and pain.

"I'll—I'll—baw!—I'll—b-r-r-r—'ll! baw!
—I'm burnt!— b-r-r-r — 'll — you'll see I'll
take you with me to-night;—see if don't!
I'll take y'—b-r-r—Hell!—'ll—by God this
very night! Come here!—b-r—damn you—
here!"

Delissa was out of the one door as Sidon's
bald head appeared inquiringly at the other;
but the girl tripped upon the stepping-stone,
and, stumbling, fell against a man's bosom.
She gave a horrified shriek, supposing the
bosom Sidon's, but heard in an instant her

husband's voice, and stopped short, as if turned to stone.

Nicholas, with a long string of bass, trout, and catfish on a hickory withe in the one hand, and his rifle in the other, sprang across the threshold, shadowed by General Floyd.

"What does this mean?" cried Nicholas, as he caught fair sight of Sidon majestically entering from the shed, and Ball, drenched and dripping, with the broken china and dish-pan—which he knew so well—on the floor.

Ball's eyes dashed hither and thither, angrily and fearfully, but he made no answer.

"D'liss, what 's this mean?" shouted Nicholas, roughly.

"Oh, kill him—kill him!" cried the girl from outside, with tears of rage in her voice. This was all the evidence and all the answer required by Nicholas

He cocked his gun. General Floyd heard the snap, and, without a word, fell across the

long barrel of the rifle with both arms, hanging with his entire weight upon it and hug-
ging it to him. Nicholas swayed with the
boy's weight; at the same instant Ball turned to the door leading into the shed.

"Let go!" shouted Nicholas, wrestling
with the boy. General Floyd gritted his
teeth and hung on. "Let go! let go, ye little rat!" yelled Nicholas.

Ball's hand was on the latch; but Sidon,
seeing the struggle that was taking place,
and judging how it must soon end, had
thrown his long body with all the haste possible in the same direction. The two col-
lided; their hands fumbled for the latch;
and the next instant Nicholas, with no time
to pick and choose, and laying about him
for a weapon of any sort, was upon them, in
his right hand the yard's length of bass and
catfish on the hickory withe. He set one
foot against the opening door, and fetched
the entire string of fish down, with a sousing
smack, upon Sidon's bald head.

It was a dangerous weapon, however for-
tuitous the choice of it, for the bass were
large and the catfish had spikes, sharp as
needles and stiff as steel. Nicholas kept his
foot against the door, and repeated the blow.
Sidon yelled in response. Nicholas hit again;
while Ball, safe enough on the other side of
his tall brother, was engaged in levering with
a broom-handle, which he had jammed into
the crack of the door. Nicholas gave another souse to the bald head vainly dodging
about, back towards him, and this one was
heavier, as the weapon came more to hand.
Sidon sank with a loud cackle of pain; and
his movement uncovered Ball, who, before
he could extract his broomstick, was taken
full swing across the face by twenty pounds
of fish. He staggered, blinded and stung,
but dragged his broomstick out notwith-
standing, and began, with as much celerity
as any monkey, to dance and dodge about
the room, using the handle as a weapon of
offence, poking and stabbing Nicholas in all

quarters, and when possible in the centre of the stomach.

This lasted but for a few seconds, when, after an unusually happy poke, responded to by a hard grunt from Nicholas, Ball made a dash at the door. Unfortunately, Misery, who had hitherto been cowering in a corner, was at that moment himself bent on instant escape from the danger of all these flying feet and swinging fish, not to say from the General, who, nearer to him, had extracted a still burning brand from the fire, and was preparing to sell his life dearly. Ball, dashing at the open door, outside of which stood Delissa spellbound, trod full on the cat, and of course fell, cursing deeply. The General, who was still between him and the door, shut, bolted, and placed his back against it. He then flourished his firebrand in a flaming circle.

Sidon was risen by this time, his bald head bleeding profusely, and was about to open the back door again, when Nicholas,

seeing Ball slip and go down, caught the tall
Saint by his long coat-tails, and swept him
across the entire cabin; he reeled over Ball's
prostrate form, kicking him in passing, and
brought up heavily upon both the General
and Misery.   Misery was by this infuriated
beyond respect of persons or power of mercy;
he accordingly sank both claws and teeth in
Sidon's hands, at the same time that the General, in no small fear for his personal safety,
rammed the glowing brand against the pit of
the Saint's stomach.   Sidon arose to the occasion; he dashed cat and brand at once to
the floor, and at the same instant that his
mate succeeded in rising under the swashing
blows he was still getting, the elder, either
in blindness or desperation, bolted straight
against Nicholas.

The hickory withe of fish was no weapon
for close quarters, and for a moment Nicholas was involved in a one-handed struggle
with his antagonist, who was crazed with
both fear and pain.   Delissa was looking in

at the window in a state of real horror, and
Ball, now up, and no longer having to ward
the fish from his head and face, seized a
three-legged stool, and, carelessly disregard-
ing the boy in his rear, prepared to smash
Nicholas's skull as soon as it was still enough
to aim at, for Sidon and Nicholas were now
rolling on the wet floor, while Misery sprang
first to one side and then to the other, spit-
ting and growling, his eyes jet-black and his
red hair on end.

Sidon gave suddenly out, and fell back
prostrate; but just as Ball raised his stool
for the blow, the boy in his rear took
him across the inside of his knees with the
iron barrel of Nicholas's rifle, which he had
seized from off the floor; the blow was
swinging and heavy; the stool flew into the
fireplace; Ball himself came down with a
smack and smash upon the unavoidable
Misery; there was a stifled waul, and the
deafening roar of the rifle, which went off as
Ball sat down on it. And in the smoke,

confusion, and general entanglement of Ball,
stool, gun, dish-pan, Misery, Nicholas, the
General, and the firebrand, there was nothing
whatever to be seen and nothing to be heard,
or no more than a series of groans from
Sidon, prostrate; short, quick half-curses
from Ball; screams of a fearful delight from
the General; and the smacking sound of fish,
which now had broken loose from their
wooden hook and were flying, three or four
at a stroke, across the cabin, as Nicholas,
enraged beyond any knowledge of what he
was about, pounded at the heads he saw
dimly before him in the dense smoke and
increasing darkness of the room.

It had long ceased to be humorous for any
of those engaged. Another minute would
assuredly have brought a death with it, for
had Nicholas had a poker or a ploughshare
in his hand, now that the striking humor was
on him, he would have hammered away with
as much heart in his industry, as he now had
with nothing but loose fish for a weapon.

Sidon was flat on the floor, and very bloody.
Ball was becoming fagged. But Delissa,
more and more frightened, ran round the
cabin, and, slipping through the shed,
opened the back door into the room and
called out to her husband, at the same time
seizing him firmly by one arm. In an instant Sidon, who must have been waiting
for some such opportunity of exit, was up
and out in a most lively manner, followed
staggeringly by Ball, at whose back Nicholas
aimed heavy blows, dragging his wife across
the room with him. He now shook himself
loose as he saw the two Saints escaping,
seized his rifle from the floor, and, unbolting
the front door, pitched out into the darkness.
General Floyd, who had become apprehensive
of his uncle's mistaking him for the shorter
Saint in the faint and smoky light, was beside himself at the thought of a chase through
the night. He followed Nicholas with a yell,
and Delissa was left suddenly alone in com-
plete silence, the smoke drifting lazily out

8

of the darkening cabin into the cool night, and only Misery's claws to be heard scrabbling along the rafters of the roof.

The floor was catching fire. Delissa threw water on it, and, lighting a candle, began to look about to see what damage was done.

The Mormons, fleeing into the night, had instinctively sought the boats. They were both in the tub before either knew of the other's being there, and before reason had returned to them found themselves several yards from the bank with but one oar. It was too late to go back. The General was dancing savage dances of glee on the bank. Nicholas was running up to where Ball knew the other boat must be moored. The Saints had fronted necessity of a kindred kind before; they took their chance without even a prayer. By the time their two pursuers had pushed off and were rowing hard, Ball and Sidon had caught the current, and were riding the swift undulations of the Big Thunder at a reckless pace.

They scarcely knew their own danger, and
this made the chase a longer one.   But its
end came: about a mile below the bend of
the river, at the foot of the second rapid,
they were overhauled in calm water, captured, and taken on shore.

In the colloquy they held on the bank, the
two Mormons standing wretchedly before
them—scalded, burnt, clawed, bitten, beaten,
wet, and wounded with catfish—and Ball
now having his hands tied rudely together—
the General was imperative in his demands.
He'd burn 'em about half dead and let 'em
go!   He'd burn their feet off 'em ;—or he'd
burn their thievin' hands, if nothing else ;—
they ought to have their eyes knocked out;
—come a-foolin' about a man's wife ;—what
did they think a wife was for?   He'd teach
'em ;—if they ever played such tricks to his
wife he'd feed 'em on red-hot horseshoe
nails !

"Let's bleed 'em," said he at last to Nicholas, with his jack-knife in his hand.   But

Nicholas was really concerned only that they should be properly run out of the country. He set about devising some method, therefore, which would render it impossible for them to make a forced march that night and escape the wrath of the neighborhood. Take them back to his house he would not! He ended by taking their boots, coats, trousers, and pocket-knives from them. They were then left to do what they pleased, and go where they wished.

" Kind o' tethered 'em, hain't ye?" said the General. "Barefoot tether!" and the exhilaration which this act of tether and freebooty caused the General was only tempered by his disappointment in that they were not at least a little roasted or bled.

The man and boy returned home. Nicholas said to his wife that he hadn't supposed she'd been in the habit of having so many strange men around in his absence, and he reckoned it wasn't an idea he could get used to.

Delissa spoke up courageously and made a clean breast of the whole matter—the cooking, her misery over it, the help Ball had been, her fears and her unhappiness, and finally, after every explanation possible, asked him for his forgiveness.

Nicholas was touched; but he was angry too. He gave it to her, he said, but after such a piece of false-appearing, such deceit and lies and all—well, he didn't know as he could feel forgiving.

He sat down, however, and ate of the fish which his wife had prepared against his return.

The next morning the General took the garments of the Mormons, and, cutting cross-sticks, made them into most direful scarecrows—entirely for his own amusement. He planted them firmly in the meadow, at some distance behind the house, placing them in such proximity and position with regard to one another that they appeared to be holding hands — and thus they waved in the wind, looking black, degraded, and melancholy.

Later on in the day, a rainy and cold one, Nicholas and the boy rode over to Carr's Mill and told their tale. Nothing had been heard or seen of the Saints. Amri Carr thought they ought to be more lessoned than they had been; lathered with fish seemed to him light enough for such seducing hypocrites. A couple of dozen men, chiefly young, but headed by Nicholas and Amri in person, were presently gathered together and scouring the woods. The Mormons were come upon towards evening. They were in a wretched and pitiable state. The feet of both men were badly wounded, and the night and morning of almost freezing rain had absorbed much of their vitality.

Amri told the two of them that they must prepare at once to depart out of this sinful world. A coil of rope was laid at their feet. With this before their eyes they both confessed that they had fallen into sin. They

" THE MORMONS WERE COME UPON TOWARDS EVENING "

begged hard for life, and Sidon chattered so
lugubriously in making his appeal, that Amri
suddenly took human pity on him, and having had a fire lighted, warmed him up with
whiskey out of his own flask.

"Spry ye up some for your own under-
taking!" was his cheering remark.

But their deaths were not intended. As
soon as the whiskey had restored their cir-
culation, a bag full of old clothing was produced. Shoes — in the shape of moccasins
which General Floyd had himself cut out
of skunk-skins—old, tattered coats, and a
couple of pairs of meal-bag trousers were
found for them, so that, as Amri said, "If
they weren't shod with humility, they were
with a skunk-skin moc'sin, which he jedged
to be pretty nigh to t'other; and if they
weren't clothed in sackcloth and ashes, they
were in burlap—ought to do for a Latter-Day
Saint!"

They were separated finally, and ridden
forty miles away, facing the tail of a mule,

and deposited at the side of the road to go whithersoever their desires might point.

During the day following " Barr's squall," as Amri christened the proceedings of that evening, Delissa was an unhappy woman ; and when her husband, returning at night-fall, preserved the same countenance and demeanor of disapproval and moody sus-picion, Delissa fell into a state of despair. Twice, and a third time, she attempted, going to him, to take all the blame in the world on herself, asking him again to forgive her and begging him to remember that, de-ceit as it had been, she had not lied to him directly.

This effort to mollify him and bring him to some reason was not successful. Do what she would, even when he saw her getting paler and losing the happiness out of her face, and at night heard her sobbing in the shed outside while he ate his dinner in si-lence and alone—with all this and more, Nicholas was unable to change the current and motion of his thoughts, and this current set all to jealousy and to suspicion, and a miserable sense of things being broken that could never be mended.

The girl suffered poignantly. It is true she had no longer any fear of Red Dolly; for that matter, as well as where her husband had obtained so many dinners, had been explained to her by the General. But, on the other hand, she felt that Nicholas no longer loved her.

What had come upon him she could not understand. She tried to lead him to explain his state of feeling. But his state of feeling was just what her husband could least in the world explain. All that he knew was that he was justifiably indignant.

It was ridiculous that his wife couldn't cook—had he not taught her? Besides, she was a woman; she must know how! And because she couldn't, she must invite a pair of Mormons into the house, and see them every day. Not a word to him! And he ate the meat that this preacher cooked! It wasn't possible to live, after that, as if it had never happened. He would forgive her; he had forgiven her; he did forgive her; but she would have to suffer, all the same, for what she had done.

These thoughts passed through his mind. He felt surly and dissatisfied. The affair had left a bad taste in his mouth.

After some days of this life, Delissa, who saw no sign of a break ahead, began to order her mind somewhat differently. Nicholas was carrying things too far. She was not the only person to blame. It had all risen out of smoke—kitchen smoke at that! Why had he not taught her, or had his sister down to teach her, to cook? If she had slipped into doing wrong, she was sorry; you couldn't be more than that. It was outrageous that he didn't forget the whole affair. To be sullen about what? Hadn't she scalded the Saint? What more could any man's wife do?

Delissa argued thus with herself, going about all the while with a dead weight in her bosom and her feet like lead.   Yet she cried no more, and ceased asking Nicholas to forgive her.   She cooked during this week in a way that would have choked an ostrich.   But her husband swallowed doggedly whatever was placed before him.   This gave him a return of heart-burn, and heart-burn increased his ill temper considerably; but he said next to nothing.

The days passed heavily over them both.

It was the early May.   The snows had long melted; the ice was gone; the rivers flowed smoothly down to the sea.   The flowers were white and blue along the sunny banks.   The sap began to stir in the roots of the forest, the buds to swell, and the leaves to unfold once more.   The air was warm, like breath; the breezes blew lightly over the earth, and the cries of birds passing again to the north dropped down through the sunny air.   The fish leaped from the river, glittering, into the sun. The deer trooped through the forest, the fawns and the does together. The sun sprang up after each night out of clear dawn ; the first beams that he touched the earth with were warm. And the mists that lay heavy and white, following the river-beds, arose at his bidding and left the earth, and lightly ascended into the heaven, and, caught by the upper winds, were swept to the east as clouds, or dissolved and passed away in the hot embrace of the sun. The world was awake and alive again.

And on one of these May mornings Delissa went down to the river to draw water. It was shortly after sunrise. As she stood on the shingly beach, and felt the warmth of the sun on her face and arms, and heard overhead the conking of the wild geese, she felt, with a start, how utterly all pleasant, natural things had passed out of her life.

When in former days spring had come, Old Sammy had always put a full bottle in his breeches pocket, and taking his little

daughter by the hand, had gone out with her into the fields and woods. They had fished together from sunrise to sundown; eaten their lunch on a log; and Delissa had enjoyed herself watching Old Sammy's bob, gazing up into the sky and looking down on the green earth, and they had talked; and each of those days had been as long as seven now. The new green was on the trees, the new life in the air, but there was no new happiness.

Three wild ducks curved swiftly down the Big Thunder, and dropped in the water near the island. Delissa followed them with her eyes, and as they splashed into the water she took a determination, sudden, but of no small moment.

Nicholas was returning late the same afternoon from a trip up the Greenleaf Road. When he reached the river, he dismounted from his mule, and hallooed for Delissa to pole the flat-boat across.

The girl came quickly down to the beach.

She first of all tied the tub to the great raft, laying a knife, with the blade open, on the boat seat ; then bared her arms and swung the raft into the stream. Nicholas wondered why she tied the tub to the raft.

As her husband watched her poling, and saw the sun on her yellow head and slim, long arms, and observed the easy way in which she made the unwieldy craft obey her, he felt a pang of compunction ; he was sorry he had been so severe ; to-morrow he would say as much—after breakfast.

He was about to take the pole from his wife, but she said she liked the fun of it. Nicholas went to the stern end and stood beside the mule. He thought it odd his wife should make such a wide circle. And what in the world was she cutting as close to the island as that for? He called to her; but the girl, although she was facing him, made no reply; she was throwing all her weight on the pole. They were nearly broadside to the current, and Delissa was holding straight for the island. If they continued on that course they'd be shipwrecked, mule and all. Nicholas made a step forward; as he did so, the girl dropped the pole again into the water and threw her weight upon it, giving the heavy raft a last vigorous shove towards the small rocky cove which she had once used as a mirror. It was about ten feet away. Nicholas, fearing the shock would upset the mule, ran forward, and would have wrested the pole from his wife, but he was too late. As he made the dash towards her she threw the pole in the river, and slipping lightly into the tub, cut the rope that tied it to the raft with the knife she had left on the prow seat, and pulled away up current with all her might. The raft struck with a crunch on the low edge of rock; the mule staggered, staggered again, and finally half fell, half plunged, into the water. Nicholas leaped as the raft struck, and finding himself in water up to his waist, pushed the raft off the rock, and as it swung round in the powerful current and brought up broadside against the lower bank, where it hung safely in an eddy, he looked up to find Delissa.

She was some yards away, and rowing further away. The pole was bobbing up and down, already twenty or thirty paces below the island, in the swifter beginnings of the rapid. Nicholas shouted to his wife. Seemingly she did not hear him, for though she was sitting with her face to him and rowing vigorously, her glance was directed a little off from the island and to one side.

He shouted again and threw up his arms. He could see her plainly enough. Her face was warmed with the exercise, for she was bracing herself against a powerful current. But otherwise, except for this suffusion of color, her expression appeared to be happy and about as usual. Nicholas shouted a third time, bellowing with all his might. Delissa gave no sign that she heard him, or that she knew that the pole was floating down stream, or that the mule was still plunging about in efforts to mount the steep and slippery side of rock, or that her husband was shouting to her and waving his arms, or that she had stranded him there and left him no means of getting away. If anything, her husband thought, she looked a shade more unconscious than usual. As he stood there, after calling the last time, a dream-like sensation came over him: he felt that he could not possibly see what he saw; and this was followed, as he continued to look after his wife in the boat and as she grew more distant each moment, by a sense that an unexpected force had jostled the order of the universe, and it was changing—had changed, all in seven or eight seconds or so. He felt, with a shock and a giddiness—although in the dullest, dumbest way possible—that the laws of nature were suspending themselves, and he was being left high and dry in the suspension. There was his wife; there the mule; here, he!

He saw Delissa beach the boat, lay aside

9

the oars, put the knife in her pocket, walk slowly up the path, and disappear in the cabin to the left.

Nicholas, could he have thrown his emotion into reasonable form, would have declared that it was no miracle or exception, but a general and incomprehensible aberration and going astray of nature in her entirety.

The mule had scrambled up the rock. To rescue himself from this lost sensation, Nicholas turned and looked about him. There was not a stick above the thickness of a switch on the island. The pole gone! He had made the raft with his own hands; not a timber in it would budge for anything less than a sledge-hammer and a nail-driver. Even his jack-knife was not in his pocket. The fancy passed fleetly through his mind that his wife was mad. He must get to shore somehow; but the river ran too swiftly either side of the island to swim it. He could try a straight line to the cabin from the end of the island; but, on second thoughts, no!

Even in a boat it required the hardest pulling for the first thirty yards. That he could make head against that first current, swimming, naked or not, he more than doubted. Surely Delissa—he guessed she must have gone off her head! All the more reason to get across. He sat down to think about it. An hour passed.

Nicholas dragged the raft upon the beach as far as he could; it was too heavy for one man to handle on dry land. He looked it over; not a timber but was fixed firmly in its socket; he concluded to burn one, so that it would fall away from the rest. By still further burning this one, he would narrow it down to a pole, or near the dimensions of a pole. But he discovered that he had only three matches in his trousers pocket, and these were wet. He laid them carefully on a rock to dry and sat down to think it over. An hour passed. The smoke began to as-

cend from the "kitchen" cabin. The smoke
meant dinner. Twilight fell. His wife was
mad, of course. The Mormons had wrought
that!

About nightfall, as he was still sitting on
his rock, and looking at his own two cabins
and at the two Mormon scarecrows up the
meadow, and wondering, with a vague sense
of surprise at his own absence of feeling in
the matter, how mad his wife was, and if the
remoter cause was not Old Sammy's bottle,
he saw Delissa come quickly down the bank
and get into the tub. She was rowing towards him! The mule had pricked her ears;
she now broke into a bray of loud satisfaction. Nicholas arose. Delissa changed her
course suddenly; she rowed across to the
Greenleaf side, and disappeared up the bank.
Mad! mad undoubtedly! She appeared, however, again, and some one with her: it was
Amri. Delissa was speaking to him. They
sat down, Amri in the stern. His jolly red
face was plain, dark as it was becoming.

Nicholas saw that this was his last hope. He shouted, throwing his voice through the steady roar of Big Thunder. Apparently Amri could not hear him. He raised his voice again, and, drawing in a deep breath, gave out a volume of sound upon " Oh—h, Amri!" which, despite the drowning noise of the rapids below and above, must have carried three times the distance. " He must ha' heard!" said Nicholas, aloud.

Amri's back, as the girl rowed him over, was slowly turning towards him. He was about to shout once more, when the thought occurred to him : Amri couldn't be deaf, for he saw Delissa talking to him; but—was he, Nicholas himself, in just his right mind? He was sure he was. But not as sure as he would have liked to be.

Amri disappeared in the cabin. He must be taking supper with Delissa. When he crossed to the other side to go home it would be dark—too dark for Amri to see him.

The darkness fell and it became night.

There was a warm, red, flickering glow out of the kitchen window. The stars had come out. Nicholas felt chilly. He was wet from his waist down.

It had not occurred to him before that he might have to pass the night on the island. He now set about making the best of it. He took off his trousers and socks and wrung them out. Pulling them on again, he began a search for a comfortable bed. In the twenty yards of its length and ten to fifteen of its breadth, the only spot not dislocated and roughened by rocks was the sandy beach. This was wet. Nicholas walked up and down this beach for some time, staring vainly across at the light in the cabin window.

She was mad! and Amri hadn't seen it on her; but why hadn't he *heard?* The idea that there might be something the matter with him, Nicholas, began now to assert itself, at first unobtrusively, shyly; but presently it seemed to gather confidence and an air of reason.

"I hain't daft, I hain't!" said Nicholas, still walking up and down the beach, and speaking aloud, "say what ye've a mind to!— hain't!  I did hear Amri tell of a man that went cracked — thought he was always in some other place from where he was; reckoned he was somebody else, too—and was that reasonable about it you couldn't prove a gol thing to him!—My name's Barr; more'n that, I am Barr."

This at first seemed conclusive.  But presently he felt that it was very odd indeed that he, Barr, should have such things befall him —that he was where he was, or where he thought he was; and, too, his mind began to revert to the past.  All the last three weeks had been of a nature that—that—well, they hadn't certainly seemed like any other weeks; and he himself—he, Barr—he hadn't seemed to himself, to Barr, as much like Barr, as much like the Barr that Barr was accustomed to know and deal with, as he, Barr himself, would like to have done.  That former Barr

—the Barr of better days—had never been unkind to a woman; not even to the first Mrs. Barr, who, Heaven and the former Barr to witness, had been a trial. He'd never been sulky or unhappy in those times. All the Mormons in the world couldn't exactly, somehow, account for that! He wasn't a changed man; he was another man; and here he, this other man, this later, unhappier Barr, sat—or at least he thought he sat here; if he didn't, somebody did! And he knew it wasn't the first Barr, for the first Barr was happy.

He might be who he would—he was a man sitting there, cold and wet. It wasn't very sound to say so—whichever Barr he was, he certainly was one, and a man—but assuredly it began to appear to him that he was two people inside of himself: One was cold and was having the hell of a time, and the Other didn't care a damn whether he was or not. And this Other One sat somewhere else, outside of all the trouble, and was nasty if he pleased to be, and said things—who the devil was *that* Barr?

Nicholas felt, as he shivered from cold, that he must stop these thoughts. He went over to the mule and patted her. He felt more himself after that. About an hour later, finding the mule lying down among the briers, the idea occurred to him that he might just as well share her animal warmth; he accordingly lay down, first tenderly stroking the object of his apprehension, in the only position possible, namely, between the beast's legs. He reposed here in a cramped position about an hour in safety. But either he made a careless motion or else the mule objected to sharing her animal warmth; at all events, she struck out in the dark, and Nicholas found himself at some distance, in a patch of greenbrier, and with a sense of having had two tons of coal fall on his back.

He said nothing whatever. But he lay alone for the rest of the night.

Day dawned, chilly and gray. The sky was cloudy. Before sunrise it began to rain.

Nicholas was hungry, and sore from the mule's treatment. It seemed to him also, as the mule whinnied hungrily at him, a peculiar aggravation of his already sufficient misery that this chattel and beast of his first wife's should have acted as she had during the night.

The day moved slowly, and Nicholas began to experience, as his hunger increased in sharpness, a reaction from the listlessness and mental confusion of the night before. He felt alert in mind, and able to endure anything. He warmed himself by jumping up and down, and throwing his arms about, under and over his shoulders.

For two hours before noon and for two hours after the rain fell in torrents. It slackened then, and presently the clouds were lifting. As this happened, it grew colder, and the man was obliged to clamber up and down

the rock in order to keep warm. It soon became out of the question to do so. His
clothing was too wet; he grew colder every
moment, and began to suffer from his
thoughts. When he tried now to face the
situation, and to realize that he, Nicholas,
was here on a rock, drenched, hungry, cold,
deserted by his wife; that this wife was mad,
or he was; or, if not that, then one of *him*
was—at all events, that he, a man, Barr,
might have to die there, or risk the forlorn
hope of swimming the rapids:—when he faced
these facts his mind balked at them ; he felt
himself grow giddy; the world of reality,
so stern and steadfast upon all other occasions, seemed to him to tremble, quiver, and
melt into a mist of absurdity and inconse-
quence.

A little later on his mind gave up the
struggle. It no longer made the slightest
effort to realize anything; it acquiesced in
the facts of the case. He found himself
thinking it as natural as possible to be where

he was and as he was; it seemed to him he had been there a year. He was beginning to feel numb with the cold, when he thought he saw a man in the dense brushwood at the far end of the meadow. There were two of them. Nicholas started up and was at once in high hopes of relief. But an hour passed without any further appearance. At the end of the hour, and as Nicholas was still staring in expectancy, his jaw dropped, his eyes widened, he caught himself by both legs, and, breathing fast, gave himself a slap on the forehead.

"'Tain't so! 'Tain't them two—again? I'm a goner: I see nothin' as it is."

He winked as he continued to gaze. The two Latter-day Saints came out from behind the cabins, holding stools in their hands. Delissa was between them. Nicholas noticed that the General's scarecrows had disappeared; but they were not merely gone— the two Saints were draped in them, as before. He had no recollection of whether

"IT SEEMED TO HIM HE HAD BEEN THERE A YEAR"

the scarecrows had been wanting for an hour
or for all the morning.

Nicholas staggered as he looked. He shut
his eyes a moment, and then, opening them
wide, stared across the river. He heaved a
deep groan.

"'Tain't so!—but 'tis! I'm cracked—
sprung! Oh, I'm loose! God-a-mighty,
what a thing to see!"

He made his way slowly up the island.
When he had reached the bushy crown of
the rock, he turned about with a sad look on
his heavy, large face.

The sun had just come out from behind
an enormous white cloud, and shot a broad
shaft of light down, illuming the green
meadow, and presently the two cabins and
the bank of the river.

Delissa was now seated on a stool, on the
grassy bank which glittered in the sun; on
her left, close to her, sat Mr. Li Ball; a little
farther off, on her right, Dank Sidon, his
long legs crossed one over another. Delissa

had her violin and bow in her hand. Both the men had their backs turned towards Nicholas, and were facing Delissa.

Nicholas propped himself against a wet rock; he swallowed two or three times, and seemed to gather himself together, keeping his eyes upon the ground at his feet.

" Now be yourself, Nic! Seein' is seein'!"

He lifted his eyelids and looked once again. He could see the three people more distinctly than at first, because of the sunlight. Delissa had on her blue dress. It was tucked up for work; her yellow hair, looser than usual, fell over her shoulders; her arms were bared to the elbows, as if for washing; and she was now playing the violin, of which, on account of the noise of the waters, no sound could reach Nicholas.

He could see nothing of the men's faces. But he made out that Ball was restless on his stool, and that his hands were flying about in a crazy sort of fashion.

Sidon sat without a motion. Nicholas

had forgotten that he had such breadth of back; but then he had never fairly seen either of them when they were clothed.

He at length threw his hands in the air, with a gesture of giving up everything, once for all.

"Same durned ident'cal palaverin' Mormon spew-trash. Look at 'em! Is that ghosts? Is that nothin'? Is them two smoke? Air? Things that ain't so? That's the little chunk, and that's the baldheaded worm: them's them, and yon's her. I'm myself: I see."

At this point in the realization of his own sanity of vision and brain, Nicholas, gazing steadily, saw Delissa lay her violin aside, and at the same moment Ball leap from his stool and embrace the girl, somewhat suddenly and roughly, but in a fashion nothing less than impassioned.

Nicholas's heart pumped a bucket of blood into his head in about five seconds; and in another moment he found himself in the Big Thunder, striking out and kicking with might and main, the current bearing heavily against him.  He swam with all the force he had; but the tide of the river was too strong to stem.  After a very few minutes, Nicholas, under the influence of violent exercise and an achingly cold bath, recovered his reason, and allowed himself to swing back to the island.

Without once looking round, he walked, dripping, to the farthest point of the rock, facing from his cabin and towards the turn of the river, and there sat down, with his back to the performance on the bank.

He knew now that he was himself well enough.  After half an hour he spoke, deliberately, aloud:

"Matter with me is, I'm a fool.  I've just done this thing to myself—just plum cut my own throat.  Might ha' known Delissa couldn't cook; might ha' had Reuben's wife come and lessoned her some, first thing; might ha' done anything sensible!  Matter

is, I've treated her like a dog! Why didn't
I forgive her when she asked? Why didn't
I kiss her, and say, 'Sho! forget it?' Why
didn't I—?"

Nicholas, at the end of an hour, was in
the condition of mind where he seemed to
himself to have done everything wrong and
nothing right since the day he allowed his
mother to bear him; especially, however,
he blamed himself for his sullenness and
suspicion in the last few days, for of
course that was the cause of his wife's
action. He now supposed her to be quite
mad, or in the nature of mad, and he was
the cause!

If he could take only a couple of steps
back into the past, and turn and make a
fresh start in time from thence. But the past
was like a wall that built itself level behind
your last heel-track, and be darned to ye if
you could even edge back a hair's-breadth!
Nicholas shook his head. Had it not been
for his devouring hunger and the numbness

of cold, he would have felt the most violent grief.  As it was, he felt that he would feel it later on.

Had he looked around, as now the sun began to sink, he would have seen Delissa laying the oars in the tub, while Ball danced wildly on the bank above.

Delissa's face was grave and drawn.  The corners of her mouth turned down, and she had a look as if she doubted not but that the next moments would bring forth some ill thing.

"Come along now, General; quit your flummaxin' about !"

It was the voice of Amri Carr proceeding from under the hat and from above the coat-collar of Sidon.

General Floyd, who was dancing with hideous violence on the bank, to keep his youthful body warm in the wet clothes of Li Ball, dashed down to the boat.  He sat down, the little Saint's seedy black hanging loosely about his limbs, the sleeves too long, and the hat falling down over his nose and ears.

Amri pushed the boat off, and in another moment they would touch the island.

" Oogh !   Bet Nic's cold !" whispered the boy, with his teeth in a chatter.

Delissa seemed to grow pale.

" He's learned a mighty smart lesson," said Amri, as he ran the boat up on the sand.

Delissa nodded to Amri to go across to where they could see Nicholas was sitting with his back still turned.

Amri and the General went across.  The girl stayed in the boat, her back turned to the island and to her husband, resting her face on her hands, shivering and trembling all over as if with cold.

" I wish I hadn't done it, now—I wish I hadn't, wish I hadn't !"

Her teeth chattered and broke the words. Reaching the far end of the little island, Amri laid a hand on his friend's shoulder.

"Rise up, Nic; come over to your woman."

Nicholas, looking up, took the situation in at a glance.

"You 'ain't been playin' the fool up and down here, hev ye?" said Amri, with a kind of blustering sternness. "G' over to her; say you're naught but a man; and man's a fool, as God made him, so help ye! Go; make your 'mends."

Nicholas got up stiffly, with the same look of penitence and sorrow. The discovery that he had been hoaxed appeared to have no effect upon his change of heart. Amri, taking a look at him, relaxed suddenly into something of his accustomed joviality.

"Darned if your Creator ain't playin' a mighty square game with you, Nic Barr! Mark my words, He don't always undertake to play so square."

Nicholas went across to the boat.

Amri and the boy engaged themselves with the mule and the raft.

As her husband approached from behind, Delissa heard his footsteps. She caught her breath once or twice and closed her eyes. Nicholas stepped into the shallow water beside the boat.

"Forgive me, D'liss."

Delissa made no answer. Her eyes were tightly shut. Her husband groaned.

"I've done wrong a heap; I was mighty crabbed and cross — I know I made you mis'able. But if you have any love left in your heart for me, D'liss—why, just say it."

Delissa sat rigid as an axe-handle; but she gave a sob, and then suddenly, without moving her head, stretched her arms out to the man bending over her, much as if she had been a little child; and rising from her seat at the same moment, she leaned towards him. Nicholas caught her as with the shifting of her weight the boat tipped and spilled her out. He lifted her up and kissed her face, which was wet with tears. Delissa sobbed again and again.

"Oh, Nic, I want to be forgiven my own self—please, please do!"

The tub had begun to float away, and as the girl had stepped deliberately into the river, they both found themselves standing up to their ankles in water.

The General made a dash at the boat, which was floating round the island.

"Y'ever see a man get with a woman," said he to Amri, as he captured it, "without he made a fool of himself? Burn me if I want to be a man, if every time I meet my wife I lose my senses. Can't he kiss her and grab the boat with the other hand? What's the pleasure of their standin' up to their knees in ice-water fur?"

"It's awful cold," said Delissa, shivering, through her tears, and drawing one foot out of the water. "Let's get out."

Nicholas set her on the little sand beach.

"May I never see light again," said Amri, "if I didn't tell that man," pointing at Nicholas, "that you couldn't cook—not enough for a—for to make rations for a grasshopper! And what's his answer? Why he said you had a face! Just as if a woman cooked flapjacks with her face!"

Amri laughed in his huge way.

At supper Delissa would say nothing. Nicholas learned from Amri of his wife's scheme to bring him to reason, and of the General's plan of wearing the scarecrows— but Nicholas cared to hear no more. He was content with things as they were. He promised his wife that he would drive her to Mrs. Reuben's the next day. They would bring Mrs. Reuben back with them to stay for a fortnight.

"Well," said Amri, as he pulled off his boots and prepared to retire to his couch of a bear-hide stretched on the kitchen floor— "well, I say let a man be a man. Let him be just as dangerous as a wild pig. If he wants a woman, let him take her—root, hog, or die! But what's that got to do with bawlin' about Solomon and all his hundreds of cucumbers!

—Begosh! as sure as a hog's a hog, a Mormon's one!"

The next morning, after breakfast, Delissa came up to Nicholas. She looked fresh and pink.

"Nic, don't you think we might take a holiday—just to be happy in?"

Nicholas thought they might.

"If we—couldn't we—well, it would be nice if we—do you think we might?"

Nicholas, after a moment or two of puzzlement, laughed suddenly, and said he thought it would be just the thing. He went back to the cabin to fetch the fishing-tackle.

They started before the sun struck the water.

"Nic," said Delissa, as the boat glided down the swift current, "I'm just awful happy!"

# ALFRED'S WIFE

CARR'S MILL stood opposite that point where the Squeeter and Somerdale roads met and crossed. Whichever of those roads you took, making for Carr's Mill, you had ten or fifteen miles of unbroken forest to go through, until, as you began to descend towards the mill, you saw it lying beneath you, in the midst of green meadows. Through these green meadows the Big Swift flowed placidly.

Next to the mill stood Brown's store. The mill was old and ramshackle, and leaned perilously; moss grew on its roof; and the dust of the flour, whitening it everywhere, gave a look of soft and withered age which brought it into fine contrast with Brown's store. The latter was of new pine boards, and looked spick and span, and even jaunty.

You expected to see Brown step prosperously out, with his hands in his pockets, whistling a waltz; but when Brown stepped out it was otherwise, for he was thin and pale and dejected; he seemed to have undergone premature dry-rot, and there exhaled from him a faint odor of staleness, much as if he had been born and reared under the glass-case with his own candies. When he walked he fell forward, first upon one spindle leg and then upon the other; when he sat down it was a kind of general collapse; and except when he added up figures, which he did easily, seeming almost to take a kind of pleasure in stating "results," he had an ineffectual, heartless way of producing his voice and his ideas. Mr. Brown came originally from "old" Virginia, and would have liked to return there; but somehow or other he had got stranded in this remote quarter of the West Virginia forests, and here he complainingly remained. Amri Carr, who worked the aged·and groaning structure called by his

name, was a weighty, rubicund, jovial body,
with a roll in his gait and in his voice, and a
way of puffing his cheeks out and blowing
after each separate sentence, as if his ideas
were a fleet of ships which he sent out towards you, and which he then followed up
and sped on with a hearty breeze from his
own lips.    Carr had a wife and eleven children.    His "house," a log cabin like all the
other domiciles of the locality except
Brown's board store, stood a half-mile below
the mill.

Mr. Brown reclined on his store steps.
Below him sat Captain Dan Crossby.    The
rumble of the mill and the warm sunshine
predisposed to silence, and silence was strict-
ly observed till a man on a black mule rode
up to the store, and, without dismounting,
handed down to the storekeeper a bag of
meal.    It was payment in kind, for no one
had money in that district.

The man on the mule was a thick-set, powerful, red-faced fellow of about forty; his

jaw and cheeks were covered with short, black stubble, and his eyes were bloodshot and restless.

"Thank you, Mr. Stott," said the storekeeper. "Thank you. Come again; do. How's your folks? Well or—"

Mr. Brown's voice died feebly away.

Mr. Stott said his sister Sarah was ailing, but the chaps—meaning his three little girls —they were well enough. He jogged off up the road.

After the lapse of about five minutes, Captain Crossby spoke to the storekeeper.

"I do everlastingly have no belief in that Hiram Stott."

"No?" said Mr. Brown.

"And he knows it," continued Captain Crossby.

"Yes?" said Mr. Brown.

"And I'm not feelin' hurt any that he does," continued the captain.

"Ain't you?" said the storekeeper.

Silence settled down again.

"What in the world Alfred Bannerman ever undertook to marry with that Carr girl for, that's what worries me to see into. Can you see into that?" inquired Captain Crossby, as if this question and his former statements of his feelings were in some way relevant and connected.

Mr. Brown avouched that he could see into nothing very far; but with some feeling that this was rather weak of him, he said, with a spasmodic effort at sympathy:

"Don't it—add up—to you?"

Captain Crossby was not much concerned with sums in addition, and made no reply, but continued, with his eyes on the lessening figure of Mr. Stott:

"You'd better not fool about Alfred. If you fool about Alfred, the first thing you know he'll be in attendance at your funeral."

Captain Crossby looked slowly around at Mr. Brown, and the latter shrank perceptibly from any idea of fooling with Alfred, in the light of such probabilities.

" Now, women's women," continued Captain Crossby; "and a woman's a mis'able thing at best; they're always makin' trouble, and fussin' or cookin' up a fuss; and to marry a woman—hit's no little matter. But to marry a woman that calls herself Carr!"

Captain Crossby shook his small gray head at this desperate idea.

" They're a wild lot, you think, eh?" said Mr. Brown, tentatively, and as if he were treading on dangerous ground.

"Wild?" said Captain Crossby. "Wicked, I reckon; as wild and wicked as hawks; and I guess Alfred he wishes his wishes—I guess he does," said Captain Crossby, clearly meditating the sort of wishes he himself would be apt to wish under such circumstances.

" There's Amri," he continued. " He said to Alfred, ' Alfred, tame her, or she'll tame you!' I heard him say it the day Alfred wedded his daughter. And Alfred he just won't undertake the job."

The little old man rose and proceeded home, pondering upon Alfred as he went.

" If Alfred's mother had fed him on snake-pizen, he'd have turned it into milk and honey fust thing she knew! As for Hiram, he wants—" Captain Crossby closed his eyes entirely, and nodded his head slowly, as if possessed of the most intimate knowledge of Hiram's "wants"; and from the general ex-pression of his face as he shuffled dustily along the road one would have judged that he would have been by nothing more pleased than freely to give Hiram whatever thing it was that Hiram — always, however, in his (Captain Crossby's) estimation—wanted.


II


The next morning the captain saddled his horse and rode up to see Alfred Bannerman. Alfred lived twenty miles away. His farm

was a new clearing—his own work—lying on
the south side of the Highland Ridge. The
log-cabin was high up, almost on the sum-
mit of the great hill. Except the stable, a
heavily built shed something ruder than the
cabin, and a pigpen, there was nothing else
in the way of building. As further sign of
life there was the corn, growing meanly now,
withered in its broad blades, and turning
over; the plot where potatoes had not
flourished by reason of drought; a brown,
dull-looking field that had borne hay; and a
small, neat garden of vegetables, chiefly cab-
bages. All around this open space, filled
with stumps and, in the higher portions,
with vast, silvery-white, dead trees from ·
which the bark had been stripped by wind
and weather, and the limbs of which stood
out strongly against the blue sky—all around
this space of mountain farm lay the inter-
minable woods — maple and hickory and
oak and poplar, turning now softly into yellow — a wilderness of forest on all sides.

Through these woods Captain Crossby came,
for the Squeeter road turned east five miles
from the mill, and the rest of the way was
only a path, so called, visible to no mortal
eye but a woodman's, and not infrequently
baffling to him.

Captain Crossby tied his horse to a sapling.
As he came round the corner a tall, slim
girl, with blue eyes and a good deal of
brown hair tied loosely, her small head carried well back, as if she never cared about
looking down, came out of the cabin with a
pail in each hand. She had color, an easy
erectness of carriage, bright eyes that were
wide open and saw everything in a twin-
kling, and a light motion that seemed to carry
her without her own will, or at least without
the faintest conscious exercise of her will.
And as she moved one would have said that
every motion gave her pleasure, and that to
put her hand to her head, as she was obliged
quickly and continually to do, her hair falling, or rather bursting, out of its confine-

ment of blue ribbon upon the slightest prov-
ocation — that this, or any other slightest
movement, whether of walking or bending
down, or whatever it might be, was to her
a positive and easy delight. And as she was
a moving person, as well by necessity of
work to be done as by nature, she appeared
to be always in some state of special pleasure and exuberance of spirit. Captain Crossby greeted her. How was Mrs. Bannerman, and how was Alfred?

"I'm glad to see you," said the girl—"oh,
terrible glad! Alfred's only so to middling,
and I'm just wretched, Uncle Dan."

Uncle Dan, thus addressed, melted with
astonishing suddenness, considering his low
estimate of female character, and, shaking
her hand warmly for him, inquired what was
her trouble.

"I guess I'm my own best enemy," she
said; "but it is lonely up here—oh, it is!
It's just dead water all the time, and nothin'
seems to prosper except the baby; and no-

body ever comes here — it might be the
world's end for all we see. Now, you do need
to see a few mortals, Uncle Dan ; you do !"

The girl's eyes flashed earnestly as she
smiled at the little, silent, gray old man who
stood looking at her with his head thrown
back in a way peculiar to himself, as if he
found that position easier to retain than it
would be to lift his eyelids, and to keep
them lifted. For generally these hung down
over his eyes so far that it appeared he must
be unable to see anything beyond his own
boots ; and though, as a fact, he saw more
in a moment, without lifting his eyes, than
do most men in an hour, however wide open
their gaze may be, he still preferred, when
he had a person to look at or into, to toss
his head back, with his pointed gray beard
thrown out at an angle in front, and his gray
hair worked up by his hat into a kind of pyr-
amid behind, and to look out keenly as now ;
and not seldom to shade his eyes with one
hand while he gazed—an action which, with

the exceeding clearness of his glance, gave
to his scrutiny a penetration and purpose
that most people winced under a little, and
were apt to avoid.

But Dellah Lucinda was a Carr, and
avoided nothing. She looked at him now,
and laughed—a quick, merry, catching laugh
that began and stopped suddenly, to go on
again as suddenly and more unexpectedly
than before.

"Uncle Dan, you look at me as if I was
dangerous," said she, laughing again.

"P'r'aps you are," said Uncle Dan, showing an entire row of even, white teeth behind
his grizzled beard.

"Maybe I am," said the girl; "I hope so.
I hate these tame cats! Kitty, kitty, kitty,
kitty!"

The girl leaned down and called an imaginary kitten. The imaginary kitten (as was
clear from the girl's actions and face) came
running to the call, and was received, taken
up, and stroked in the approved way.

"And kitty comes like that," continued Mrs. Bannerman, with sudden emphasis, "and is given her milk, and she purs!" Mrs. Bannerman purred in a way that was astounding. "And she's a good kitty." Her voice caressed the virtues of the "good kitty." "And I hate that sort of tame cat, and so do you, Uncle Dan. You do—you know you do!"

Uncle Dan scarcely smiled at this sudden burst, which Mrs. Bannerman accompanied by an action of both hands, tucking in recalcitrant locks, or rather masses, of hair, one strand of which had fallen out at each movement made towards or over the too tame kitten.

"And you know you'd hate to be a woman," continued she; "and I do. And I'd a great deal liefer be a-chasin' old he-bears up in the Big Pines, and to suffer and want up there, than to live"—she looked around in every direction, nodding her head at each object she saw—"like this."

Captain Crossby retained the same position of head and body, and looked from under his eyes at the girl before him with a kind of distant scrutiny. As she spoke she had grown more earnest, and her color came and went with surprising suddenness, so that there seemed to be never a moment when the light of her entire face was not either growing less bright and fading partly away, or increasing in brightness until, at times, there was a sudden overflow in all directions, and a wave of rosy fire passed over her neck. At such moments she seemed to tremble with the excitement of her own nature; but it passed away then, and left her radiant and alive, but less astonishing; and after each such climax and rush of emotion the girl generally laughed. Her laugh seemed to say that she had felt, as perhaps you had seen, that she was being carried off her feet, but that was over now—she had regained her footing.

"The fact is, Uncle Dan," said she, more

composedly, " it's duller than death up here, and twice as unnatural. We might be dead for who we see. You have it better at the mill ; there's life there."

Captain Crossby kept his gray eyes fixed upon Mrs. Bannerman.

" How's Hiram ?" said he.

" Hiram !" cried the girl. " What have I to do with Hiram ?" She frowned slightly and suddenly at Captain Crossby. "I expect he's well enough," she continued rather defiantly ; " and if he ain't, let him mend it."

" Comes over pretty often," said Captain Crossby, stating the fact in his wisdom rather than asking the question.

" Oftener than he's wanted," said Mrs. Bannerman ; and she opened her eyes wide at the old man. " Alfred's yonder ; I must fill my pails."

Captain Crossby watched her go down the hill. She was not singing, but she seemed to be swinging the two pails to a kind of tune.

Alfred was sitting under an apple-tree in the orchard, putting a new lock on his rifle. It was an old-fashioned gun, a flint-lock, and stood as high as the man who used it. The greeting that passed was warm; for, despite their difference of age, the two men knew each other well; it was a quiet, unnamed friendship.

"You look sick," said Captain Crossby, after an examination of his friend's face.

"Out o' heart, Uncle Dan," said Alfred, looking up from his gun.

Alfred Bannerman stood six feet and odd in his stockings, and was broad and lean. He was not a very remarkable-looking person at first sight, or, indeed, at any after sight — or not, at least, until you had become aware of a serious, innocent pair of eyes in which the man as he was appeared to find some outward expression. In his long arms, his big hands and feet, his small head, with no great quantity of straight brown hair, his rather large nose, his stoop-

ing carriage and broad shoulders, there was
nothing to note different from many other
men. Neither were his eyes noticeable, save
perhaps in this, that they remained serious
while the rest of his face smiled. He was
clean-shaven—that is to say, his jaw had felt
the touch of razor about ten days before,
and glistened now with a kind of straw-
colored stubble of coming beard. It was a
good face, but it puzzled you in the very
moment of discerning its goodness and composure; for if you saw Alfred smile, as he
did now in looking up at Captain Crossby,
and thought how gentle he would be with
children, judging from the sweetness of his
expression, you at the same time felt a little
disturbed by this seriousness of his eyes. It
was not easy, you felt, to prognosticate the
actions of the man who had that innocence
of outlook upon the world; not easy to fore-
judge how far, through what entanglements,
unbiassed by what complexities, that apparently profound sincerity would carry him.

"Out o' heart," he said, and smiled at Captain Crossby, who was standing up in front of him.

"What for?" said the latter, leaning on his rifle.

"It's just this way, Uncle Dan," continued Alfred, pushing his tools to one side. "When I married Lucinda, two years now agone, I told her what she had to expect: lonesomeness, and poor living compared to what her fawther gave her, and hard times, and whatever a woman has to endure; and she said she knew what she had to expect, and I guess she made a mistake."

Alfred looked inquiringly at Uncle Dan, but the latter had taken refuge, in advance, from all such looks by shutting up his left eye and gazing with his right down his rifle-barrel, in the circular darkness of which he appeared not infrequently to find immense reserves of mystery—as if at the bottom of that long tube lay the final knot and entanglement of poor humanity.

"I guess she made a mistake," said Alfred. "At her fawther's there was brothers and sisters and mother, and friends that came in, and they as wished to keep company with her; it was a road which brought travellers, and altogether it was a lively place where a young girl might enjoy her life—which she leaves for this and me."

Alfred looked helplessly at Uncle Dan; but as the old man continued to ponder down his gun-barrel, and gave no sign of sympathy for Lucinda's loss and exchange of all the goods and gayeties of a life situated on a road "for this" — Alfred had looked about him as he spoke—"and me"— he continued:

"And this season's drought has pretty nigh to ruinated me. Corn, hay, onions, potatoes—you know how it is—everything, to the bees even, is less or nothing, and it is the pinchiest time that I do ever remember."

Uncle Dan nodded his head slowly at this

point, and Alfred continued in his slow, balanced way of speaking, as if the unhurried consideration of any subject in discussion, and of every side of such subject, and hence of every word that expressed or threw light upon it, was the natural and inevitable process of his mind. Be the subject what it might, Alfred approached it, and looked at it, handled and weighed it, with the same deliberate impartiality. When he spoke of the season being the pinchiest he had ever known, it was perfectly clear by the intonation of his voice, that he was being fair to the demands of all the other seasons to be considered more pinchy than this one.

"And it's just this way, Uncle Dan," said Alfred: "she's fallen to lonesomeness; and I wake up at night, and hear her crying and crying all in the dark; and then I try to comfort her—I try all I can. I tell her it won't last, and I tell her this and that; but you must have comfort for to comfort with.

And it's lonesome and poor and hard, and
I'm not enough for her, that's the truth,
Uncle Dan."

Alfred looked out over the hills and into
the distance, as he was apt to do when trouble came upon him heavily. As he continued, there was a sincerity in the quiet of
his manner, in his few simple gestures, and
in every intonation of his voice, that would
have prejudiced the minds of the dullest jury
in his favor, even had the evidence against
his truth been of the most final and conclusive kind.

"You may know it's pinchy with us," said
he, "when I say we killed Lucy, two weeks
back, on a Thursday."

Lucy was Alfred's pet hog, which Captain
Crossby well knew, and accordingly com-
pressed his lips, still gazing down the barrel
of his gun, as much as to say, Has it come to
this? Lucy had come into this world of
men and pigs the same day and hour that
Lucinda had plighted her troth to Alfred,

and hence—at least, in part—the regard en-
tertained for her.

"Yes ; we just had to eat her," said Alfred. "Lucinda loved that pig, and certainly she did Lucinda.   Well, I said last July,
'We must kill her;' but Lucinda she said,
'No;' and when I mentioned it last month
she burst right into tears, and cried that
hard it 'most broke my heart. But last week
I just said to her at morning bite, 'Lucinda,
I must do it to-day; it isn't right to feel too
much about a pig.'   So I took this old gun
o' mine, and I went down to the pen yonder,
and stepped into it, and Lucy-hog she came
to me just like a child and as trustful as a
pig could be!   Uncle Dan, it just cut me
like a knife.   I could not pat her, and I do
assure you I was afraid to look her in the
face.  Well, I was doubtful if I could kill her
the first shot, because, you see, this old gun
o' mine it had a bad lock, and it might miss
fire."

Uncle Dan assented, and Alfred went on

with the same deliberation and choice of words, and in the same spirit of innocent and composed seriousness.

"But I couldn't kill that pig with an axe— I just p'intedly couldn't ha' done *that!* So I said nothin' to her, Uncle Dan, but I just up and pulled trigger, and it missed. I pulled again, and it missed again; and it kept on snapping and missing, and perhaps that shook me, or what not, for when it did go off rightly, it bored that pig right through the left ear. You never did hear such a squalling and yelling, and such a hoggish row—and she seemed to look at me sort of half suspicious! And at last she came running to me—me, with the old gun smoking in my hands! And I tell you, it went right to my heart. I threw my gun down, and I got that axe from outside, and I took it into that pen, and raised it—and it was done."

Alfred heaved a heavy sigh at the remembrance.

"When I came to my senses she was dead,

12

and I saw this gun lying there. I took it up, and I thought, 'I'll break you, so you'll never play that trick again.' I got two stones—one big, one little—on the hill outside, and I laid the gun on the big one, and then I thought to myself: 'No; the gun is as good as any other gun. It's innocent. It was the lock that missed fire, not the gun.' So I took the lock off, and I laid it on that stone, and I pounded and pounded that lock until I do not believe a man could have known it was, or ever had been, a lock. I was rightly mad; I was as much angered as I ever do remember to have been."

Captain Crossby threw his head back at the close of this recital, and smiled, showing his teeth, at the thought of Alfred "rightly mad." The latter smiled, too, recognizing that there was to Uncle Dan a certain humor in the situation, which, however, was overborne for him by the tragedy and pathos of his affection for Lucy and the disaster of his relations to her at the last.

"So," said he, meditatively, "we're living on Lucy ever since."

The two men talked together for an hour or more, at the end of which time they had agreed to leave the next week for a two-months' hunt in the Big Pines. They hoped to kill two or three bear there, and twice as many deer. They could safely bring these back in the cold weather, and Alfred, with whatever else he might kill in the way of game nearer home, would be able to tide over the hard winter.

Captain Crossby was to have his half share. He would have gone with his young friend for less than that; for Alfred was a born hunter, and tilled the soil only because of the uncertainty in the returns of the chase; and this predilection of Alfred's for hunting drew Uncle Dan towards him mightily. Moreover, for some mysterious reason he considered Alfred Bannerman a "man," and seemed to find this a further and peculiar attraction in him. He himself had passed a quarter of his life's days in the deep woods, and was a bear-hunter or nothing. He knew their ways and methods, and he loved a bear, alive or dead, perhaps better than anything else on earth. He certainly respected them as he did few men and no woman. And this respect, intimacy, and knowledge of his accounted, no doubt, in the mystery of things, for a certain shuffling gait he himself had, a short, decisive grunt he sometimes gave out, and a general savageness, or at least surliness, of disposition, evinced particularly to those females most nearly related to him.

As the two men rose to go, Lucinda at the door calling them to supper, Hiram Stott came down the hill and through the orchard. He had walked over from his own place, a few miles distant.

"How d'ye, Mr. Bannerman? Stranger here, Captain Crossby. Hot? Yes, it is. Yes, it is hot."

Hiram wiped his sweaty red brow with

his sleeve. Alfred spoke to him; but from Captain Crossby he got no answer other than his looks fixed upon him.

Hiram's little eyes shot about in their red lids from one to the other, and he tried very evidently to make himself agreeable. He informed Alfred he had come to borrow some medicine for his sister. She was ill, and Alfred's wife had the medicine; her mother, Mrs. Carr, had brewed it. Might he borrow the same?

Alfred said he'd better get it. Hiram moved off uneasily. Captain Crossby's silence when he was about, and the fixed, quiet, rather dangerous attention he appeared to be giving him, embarrassed him, and heated his face. The thermometer seemed to Hiram to jump ten degrees whenever he was in Captain Crossby's presence.

As he turned his back on the two men now, his large, thick-skinned face was flushed with the heat of his walk, with this embarrassment, and with anger at it. He ran his hand through his black hair, and gave out a kind of low, discontented chuckle, as he thought to himself that it was a small matter, anyhow, what old Dan Crossby thought or didn't think of Hiram Stott.

"Alfred," said Uncle Dan, "I'm just a-thinkin' that I don't care greatly about that man."

"He's pretty poor of a man," said Alfred, "but he knows better than to let his poorness loose round here. I told him to his face—he obleeged me to do it, for he asked me my opinion — I told him that he ought to ha' been shot for killing Joe Rayner; and if not then, and for that, why, I told him he ought to ha' been shot for killing of John Allen. He fired up, and said he hadn't killed no such man. I said he had put an ounce of lead into his spine : if that was killing, why then he killed him."

"They might have knowed he'd marry the Allen woman," said Captain Crossby. "He wanted John Allen's wife, and he got her; and though I don't wish to take away any man's character, it's just my notion edzackly that Hiram Stott ain't a safe man." Uncle Dan looked towards Alfred for corroboration, and then proceeded dryly and conclusively: "And it's my opinion, too, that he's a perfect hell-sop."

This was a favorite expression of Captain Crossby's, and signified his intense moral disapproval of the person concerned, not unmixed with a strong natural antipathy; and it might be supposed to imply that—at least, in Captain Crossby's opinion—the said party had soaked up all possible depravity from the region noted in the first syllable.

The sun had sunk, and the pleasant, cool shadow of the evening had fallen on and over everything. Supper was done. Hiram was still there. Alfred had asked him in "for a bite," and he had stayed on, despite his sense of Captain Crossby's disapproval, and indeed partly in consequence of it. He felt it was necessary for him to show Dan

Crossby that he wasn't to be put down.
When he rose to go, he asked Alfred to
bring his wife over to see his sister Sarah;
he thought Mrs. Bannerman would cheer
her up. Mrs. Bannerman said at once that
unless his sister Sarah was sick to death she
couldn't go; she had her husband and child,
and couldn't leave them.

Hiram made no response, but, shouldering
his rifle, gave them good-night, and rolled
out of the house. Presently, the door being
open, they all heard Hiram call back, "If
you're any way afraid of anything, Mrs. Bannerman, don't come." Lucinda flushed, and
cried out, "Afraid o' what?" As Hiram
moved up the hill, Captain Crossby went out
of the cabin, and heard him gruffly chuckling
to himself in the dark.

When Captain Crossby had turned into
one of the two beds in the single room
which composed the entire "house," Alfred
and Lucinda went outside to talk. He told
her of the plan for the hunt in the Big Pines,

and further explained that Uncle Dan's brother would come up once a week and look after her during his absence, and that he meant to ask Lucinda's father to let her younger brother Bob stay awhile.

As he spoke, Lucinda walked away, and stood with her back towards him.

"Where are you going?" said Alfred.

"I'm just sick and crazy with bein' alone," replied his wife. "And I just hate my life, anyway."

Alfred sat down on a stump, and took the girl on his lap, gently, and kissed her.

"It will all go better when I get back, Lucy," said he; "I promise you, it certainly will."

"Never!" said Lucinda, with a wild rising inflection and a sob, and then burst into tears.

"Alfred," she said, when the first heaviness of the storm was over, "I just ain't fit to live, and you're that good to me it makes it worse."

## III

Next week Alfred and Captain Crossby made their start for the Big Pines. As they went down the hill in Indian file—two mules and half a dozen dogs, followed by the men with their long rifles—Lucinda stood at the door to watch, the tears of parting in her eyes. She mounted a stump to see them ford the Little Swift below, her dress fluttering in the breeze, her hair loose, her eyes bright, and her color coming and going, as she blew kiss after kiss to her husband. When they were gone she sat down on the stump and cried bitterly.

Perhaps no one knew how lonely Lucinda was even before Alfred's departure. She was not only that, but discontented and unhappy and sore, and wanted she knew not what. If Alfred was more than usually tender to her it made matters worse. "If he'd only beat me and beat me!" she would say to her baby, who replied by a gurgle, and a

fat fist waved in the air. But Lucinda had
at heart—it had not come there suddenly, it
had grown—a sense of some deficiency in
Alfred's nature. She expressed it to herself
by desiring that he would "beat her." It
seemed as if he was too gentle, as if he
lacked a certain positive quality, a harsh-
ness, or roughness, or what not, that would
make life easier. She wondered at times if
he would avenge an insult; if he had had a
sister betrayed, would he, like Lick Hern-
shaw, "take into" the woods after the be-
trayer, and shoot him dead three weeks later
as he was watering his horses in the Red
Deer Fork? She was not certain that he
would. And now that Alfred was gone
these thoughts and doubts, with a sense of
the hardness of life, all came upon her with
redoubled force and frequency. Her only
means of driving them away was to sing,
and sing she did. If any one had passed
between the hours of dawn and dark they
might have heard her clear, high voice sing-

ing on the hill-top, in the solitude of the woods.

Captain Crossby's brother came up twice, and then was taken with a fever, and came no more. Bob was needed at home.

Hiram came down one day after the men left, and once again; then not for a week. On his third appearance he stated that sister Sarah was dead and "coffined up" and "buried under," and that that was the completion of her sufferings. He came every day for the next week, until Lucinda told him to stay away.

It was the day after that, that the baby was taken ill. Lucinda was alone, without help. She saw the child grow worse and yet worse, and could do nothing for it. It was a severe ordeal, but of short duration. In less than four days her child died.

In the quiet that suddenly fell upon her with the cessation of the child's struggle for life, Lucinda preserved a kind of composure. She was silent; she set the cabin to rights;

she attended to whatever necessary work
she had neglected during the child's illness.

As she sat, at the close of the day, on the
stump outside the cabin, her hands in her
lap, she felt scarcely alive; a deadness had
fallen upon her, a profound apathy of life.
Her entire being lay, like her hands, passive,
grasping nothing, without even the desire of
grasping.

Hiram came late in the evening.  She allowed him to enter the cabin, but she covered the face of the baby from him.

The next day he offered to dig the grave
for her.  Lucinda refused the offer at once.
She would dig it herself, and went out to
fetch pick and spade.

"Why," said he, as she returned, "you
can't dig it, the ground's frozen.  Come
along, now; I'll pick the hole out.  Grave's
a grave.  What's the difference to *it* who
digs the dirt?"

" There's some things I'd a heap sooner

be dead than see you to do," replied the girl
in a low voice.

Hiram felt that he was nearing dangerous
ground, but some spark of natural sympathy
and desire to be helpful in such an exigen-
cy, combined in whatever degree with a determination which he had lately formed to
make himself useful to the woman before
him, impelled him further.

" Well, when you've got the hole dug, I'll
bring it up to you, if you say so ; and I can
chuck the earth back for you."

" Don't you lay a finger on my baby to
bring it up to me !"

Lucinda spoke with a gravity of manner
and with an absence of quick emotion which,
as Hiram was unused to it in her, startled
him more than the most violent exclamation would have done. He looked sullen
and confused, but made no answer.

" There's some things you have nothin'
to do with," continued Lucinda, looking at
Hiram as if she despised him—"nothin' to

do with, Alfred absent or not; and there's
things in this world that ain't fittin' to be
done. You'll let me to do as I say. It's not
your loss; and those that have lost let them
bury their loss, not another."

Lucinda went up the hill. She chose a spot
under a tall pine where she herself had frequently sat with the baby. The ground was
hard, and the digging cost her labor. The
afternoon was still and cold; but cold as it
was the girl was soon warmed with her
work. As the hard surface was broken up
and thrown out, the digging became easier,
the grave grew deeper rapidly, and Lucinda
was soon obliged to work inside of it. At
a little before sunset it was completed. A
heap of brown earth was thrown out on all
sides; and Lucinda, standing up in the grave,
could barely see the horizon, where the sun
was setting coldly in a bank of dull-red
clouds. She looked up only to measure the
depth to her satisfaction. Then she bent
down again and began to smooth with her

hands the roughness of the clay bottom. She smoothed it as if it had been the clean sheet of some small bed which had become creased and rumpled; and as her hands moved lightly over it, the sweat from her forehead dropped on the loose earth.

The sun had gone down and left the extent of winter forest, seen from the hill, lightless and cold-looking, when Lucinda began to go up the path with the child in her arms.

She laid it at the foot of the pine, where she had frequently rocked it to sleep. The same pillow she had used was under its head. It was after dark before she laid it in the grave she had prepared.

Hiram stood at the door of the cabin and listened at intervals. He could hear no sound until, about an hour or two before midnight, as he judged, he caught the click of pick and spade again, and concluded that Lucinda was completing her work in the darkness. She came down to the cabin shortly after that and threw herself upon the bed.

He knew that she had not slept at all the previous night, and guessed she could scarcely have got much sleep during the baby's illness. But now he saw her lying in her clothes on the bed opposite, sleeping profoundly. He reckoned she'd come to herself if she slept enough.

Hiram was obliged to spend the next day at his own place, and did not see Lucinda again until the following morning. When he came down into the cabin he was no less than astounded. For just so quiet and self-contained as she had been before the child's death and burial, just so wild and extravagant in her lack of self-control did she appear after these. She seemed to have buried with the child any care that she had for herself. She spoke little, and when she did, suddenly and with anger. But her gestures, her motions, the expression of her face, and everything she did, or the manner in which she

left anything undone, expressed just such a
spirit in her as would have induced her to
seek rather than to avoid a blow or a cut,
had these impended—almost such a spirit as
would have made it a relief for her to be
thrown into danger and violence, and to
suffer from them.

While she was in this state, Hiram stayed
at the cabin.  He cooked and did all the
work there was to do, his eyes growing more
bloodshot and his face redder with bending
over the open fire.

Three weeks passed thus.  The coldest days
of winter were come and the snow lay a foot
deep along the ridge.  It was a week past
the date fixed for Alfred's return.  Hiram
had been obliged to spend two days at his
home.  On the evening of the third day he
appeared with a sledge and a mule.  The
next morning, as Lucinda was splitting wood
outside the cabin, he brought the mule and
sledge to the door, took her heavy cloak
from the peg inside, and coming out with it,

threw it over her shoulders. The girl looked
at him defiantly.

"I know what you want," she cried out,
" but you're not going to have me!"

" Come on !" said Hiram, in as gentle and
wheedling a tone as was possible to him.
Lucinda laughed insultingly.

"Come on !" she repeated, imitating him.
He drew his eyebrows together, but, laying a
hand on hers, was about to say something
flattering and sweet.

" Take it away!" said Lucinda, looking at
the heavy hand covering her own.

" What's the use of makin' believe ?"—soft-
ening his voice as much as was possible for
him, and, as a consequence, speaking in a
kind of raspy whisper. " Don't you know
that ?"

" Take it away !" cried Lucinda, raising the
axe she held in the other hand.

Hiram only clasped her hand more strongly. The girl swung her forearm back, and
the axe, making a loose, wide circle, began to

descend in such an arc as, fully described, would have slashed Hiram's wrist or hand, and not impossibly both his and the woman's, beneath it.  But in an instant the helve was caught close to the head and swung out of the girl's grip.

"Cut and bite, eh?" said Hiram, in a voice quite natural to him.  At the same moment he took her about the waist and under the knees and set her down, all in one motion, on the sledge.  Lucinda attempted to rise.

"You're a-comin' home to me," said he, letting both his hands fall heavily from behind on her shoulders.  Lucinda gave a cry of pain.

"Sit there, then!" he said, warningly.

Lucinda's face was flushed, her eyes were blazing, and she looked dangerous enough; but she remained seated.

"You know what'll come o' this?" cried she, in an excited voice.

Hiram laughed rudely.  "Know?  Know?

Why, yes,"—with a sneer,—"nothin' 'll come of it."

"You can take me, for all I care," said the girl, bitterly. "Take me; it's nothing to me, nor anything else on this earth."

Hiram started the mule, walking beside the sledge with the reins in one hand and his rifle in the other.

"But killin' 'll come of it," added Lucinda. "You better forego your bargain, Hiram Stott. I may be pretty enough, but I ain't worth your life to you."

The sledge was descending the hill and the cabin was nearly out of sight.

"You'll do," said Hiram, with a look at her. "I'll be about when there's killin'. What I want, I gen'rally get," he added, with a laugh.

There was something too triumphant in the words, as in the short laugh that followed, and Lucinda half rose suddenly, and began to get off—the sledge still in motion. Hiram let the reins fall on the snow, and trail; the mule walked on, while he leaned over and dropped the barrel of his rifle on Lucinda's hand, which had caught the up-right of the sledge, and with which she was supporting her half-raised body in the act of stepping from the sledge into the snow. The iron barrel fell heavily, the hand relaxed of itself from the shock, and the girl sank back. She then lay down, covering her face with her hands, but making no sound.

The distance from Alfred's cabin on the ridge to Hiram's, low down in a swampy ground and surrounded by a host of dead-ened trees, alder bushes, and laurel, was seven miles. As they arrived at the door Hiram said, contemptuously:

"Alfred's nothin'. He's a sheep."

Lucinda, who had been for some time sit-ting upright and silent, went off suddenly into a passion of dry, agonized sobs. Hiram, fearing she might do herself some injury in the violence of the moment, knelt in the snow beside her and laid his hand on her

head to stroke her hair. She replied, with
no intermission of convulsive sobbing, with
a blow in the face too quick to be evaded.

"You may do what you will with me,"
she said, "but you can't do *that*. It's not
your business if I cry."

She got up from the sledge, and, stumbling in the soft snow as she walked, went
into the cabin, still sobbing. The children
had come to the door.

"That's your new mother, chaps," said
Hiram.

## IV

In another week Alfred and Captain Crossby came back, successful, from their hunt.
The mules were loaded with bear's-meat
and venison. There was enough for months.

As Alfred caught sight of his cabin on the
hill he felt as much pleasure in his return,

as much buoyancy of spirit and hope for the future, as he had ever known in his life.

Captain Crossby stopped at the stable. Alfred walked quickly into the cabin, the door of which stood wide open. No one was there. He called his wife's name. As he did so, he saw that the fire was dead, and, looking about him, perceived that the room was in disorder. He went to the door. There were no fresh footsteps to and from the cabin. He noted the sledge-track, now a week old. It occurred to him that Lucinda had for some good reason left for the mill, and he went inside again to find any letter there might be there for him. On the bed-quilt was pinned a piece of yellow paper. Alfred read:

Your woman's come to live with me. Why'd you leeve her to starve? The young one hit died.
HIRAM STOTT.

Alfred sat down on the bed, the bit of yellow paper in his hand. Captain Crossby

came in, and, seeing his friend's face, took
the paper. The two men looked at each
other. A flush of color appeared in the
older man's wrinkled, smoke-begrimed face,
but he said not a word. He turned to the
chimney-place and began kicking among the
cold ashes on the hearth.

Alfred was silent a long time, sitting weak-
ly, and apparently in a dazed state of mind,
on the bed. Captain Crossby moved in and
out, made a fire, unpacked the mules, cleaned
his rifle and Alfred's, and cooked supper; all
which time he said nothing, only now and
again casting a side glance at Alfred.

After one of his momentary absences from
the cabin he found the room empty when he
returned. He put down the log he had on
his shoulder, and went out, peering around
in all directions for Alfred. It was dark.
The old man had some vague fear in his
mind, for he ran round the cabin, up the hill
a short distance, and back, with astonishing
speed, glancing quickly here and there, now

stopping to listen, now bending down over
the snow, and looking, in the suddenness and
celerity of his movements, and in the way
in which he bent down as he ran up the
slippery hill-path, with his gray hair piled up
on his small head and his eyes restlessly in-
quisitive, as unlike anything purely human as
can be imagined wearing a shirt and boots.
He presently heard the snow crunch behind
the stable, and concluded that Alfred must
be there.  He stopped a few feet away.  He
could see pretty plainly, for the brilliance
of the winter stars mingled with the last
radiance of twilight, and the snow reflected
whatever light there was.  He saw Alfred
standing in the shadow of the stable, with his
face against the logs, his body moving, and
apparently shaken with some strong emotion.  He heard a succession of dull, bumping
sounds, and supposed he was kicking the
logs.  But at the same moment he saw him
raise his hands and once and again bring the
closed fists with all his force against the

wall of the stable.   The old man ran forward, and, throwing himself upon his friend, forced him away from the building.

As he did so, he saw that his forehead was bleeding profusely.

" Have yourself! Have yourself!" said he, and gripped the man by both wrists.   Alfred's hands, too, were wet with blood, and he was trembling as if in the violence of an ague-fit.

"Alfred!" said Captain Crossby, as if he would bring him to himself by calling his name to him.   Alfred made no reply other than to continue breathing rapidly, as if after violent physical exertion, and trembling from head to foot.

Uncle Dan led him into the cabin.

" That'll do !" he said, with severity.   He took a piece of rag, and, dipping it in water, sopped Alfred's bloody forehead and face. It was more bruised than cut by the force with which he had thrown himself against the logs.   But he became gradually quieter,

and in half an hour found himself eating the
meal that had been cooked for him.  When
the older man had cleared up and washed
the dishes, he threw a section of a tree on
the fire and drew his chair up to it.  Alfred
sat on the floor, with his back against the
stone chimney-pillar and his long legs out
in front of him.

"Alfred," said the old man, leaning over
and taking one of Alfred's hands gently in
his, an action probably as unusual with him
as standing on his head would have been—
"Alfred, I guess we know each other.  It's
natural you should feel as you do."  Uncle
Dan spoke with something akin to a drawl
and in rather a high voice.  "Now," he continued, "I've been a-thinkin' this matter
over, and hit's just my opinion that we must
go right down to Hiram—we must go right
down to him; for I've a notion that that
man wants to be *settled*."

Alfred looked up at his friend sadly.

" Hiram has children, and they're motherless," continued Captain Crossby; "but if he ain't settled and done with, he'll bring about more motherless and more fatherless children, too, than he has himself twic't over. Now that's what I conclude to be the case."

Alfred made no rejoinder. In a few minutes he threw himself on the bed. Captain Crossby heard him breathing irregularly and wakefully through the night.

The next morning, when they had eaten, he intimated that there never was a time like the present to do a just action. Should they go down and "settle" Hiram? Alfred was sitting in the doorway, with his head against the jamb, looking out into the distance.

"Uncle Dan," said he, "Hiram has done me grievous wrong. He'd far better have taken my life from me than her I loved. But if we kill him, it throws her out on the mercy of the snow. I don't reckon her fawther will roof her now; assuredly she shall never come under my roof again."

Alfred paused, for something stopped his speech and shook him violently. Then he continued, more brokenly and more excitedly:

"I will not kill that man—no, not howsoever I may want to do so—for he's her only chance now. But I have what I would like to say to him face to face."

Captain Crossby felt that a righteous vengeance was slipping from his grasp. It caused him unspeakable chagrin, but he agreed to go with Alfred merely to interview Hiram. The peace was to be kept.

It was a gray day, with a dense snow-fog, and everything dripping, the tree-trunks a few feet away obscure, and the distance at a hundred yards altogether lost.

They heard Hiram chopping. The strokes resounded dully. As they advanced farther they saw the figure of the man himself, raising his axe and letting it fall regularly, his body, as it swung to and fro at the work, looming up indistinct and huge in the fog.

Captain Crossby called out. Hiram was seen promptly to seize his rifle and make for the cover of a tree. From this refuge he would not hear of any parleying unless one of the two men left his weapon behind. Alfred leaned his gun against an oak.

As the two men confronted him, standing about ten feet distant, it was evident to both of them that he mistrusted their motives. Captain Crossby began the "business," as he called it, by stating that his young friend had somewhat to say to Hiram, and that he himself had merely come as a witness. Hiram replied in monosyllables, with evident distrust of every word spoken. His bloodshot eyes glanced restlessly from one to the other, and his fingers pattered constantly on his gun.

Alfred inquired first of the child's death, and received such answer as Hiram had to give. He then said, without any further preface:

"Hiram, you have wronged me, and you

know it; you have lied, and you know it. And it is not the first time you have done wrong or lied; for you are a wrong-doer and a liar from your birth to now, and you know that same to be true."

He stood looking into Hiram's angry, anxious, and not unastonished eyes with the same expression that he might have worn upon his face had he been telling a child of its naughtiness, and there was no other witness of strong emotion in his manner than a violent, quick twitching of his long fingers and a heightened color. Hiram appeared doubtful what to say or do in reply. This was plain language, to be sure; but as the man before him had left his rifle behind, it clearly could not be meant as an insult. Still, the words were not such as he was accustomed to hear, and he was about to reply in kind, as he conceived kind, when he glanced from Alfred's face to that of Captain Crossby. The distant scrutiny of the older man gave him a kind of cold shock. He felt as if Uncle Dan were sighting an imaginary rifle at him ; for one of the latter's eyes was slightly closed and the other had an open, observant look which Hiram felt to be disagreeable.

"If ye think ye can cuss me out," said Hiram, turning to Alfred, "ye are mistook."

"I'm not a-cussin' any man," said the latter ; "but I wish and I mean to say this, Mr. Stott, and I will say it clear : so long as you treat Lucinda Carr right, as a woman should be treated, you are free of me. I bear you a grudge, but I will do you no evil. I wish not to see you or her, and so far so good ; but if you evil entreat her, or desert and leave her, I will hunt you down and surely kill you, if I can lay my hands upon you—which is all I have to say."

The man thus addressed was not a little surprised by the termination of Alfred's moral lecture. The latter's fingers were holding one another, intertwined tightly, and his eyes were wide open with excitement.

Hiram gave a short, gruff laugh.

"That all?" he said.

"You might just add this from me," said Uncle Dan. "You're a man I don't completely respect, and there's nothing on this earth would give me the same pleasure as a settlement with you; and if you leave that woman, I tell you p'intedly, I never will rest until I bury your body in the ground, for you're a burden on it. Now that's just my idee edzackly."

Uncle Dan, who had hitherto been exceedingly grave in demeanor, and was sufficiently fierce in what he had just said, now threw his head back and broke out with a silent laugh, showing the row of teeth behind his beard.

Hiram glanced darkly at him.

"Guess you're both done, eh? Guess the meetin' 's adjourned, eh? Now suppose you two get off from my place."

He drew his gun into the crook of his elbow, as if he were quite ready to use it if not obeyed in this last injunction.

Uncle Dan suggested quietly to Alfred that he should return to the tree against which his rifle leaned, and cover his (Captain Crossby's) retreat; and as Alfred went back to execute this movement, the old man faced round upon Hiram once more. The two confronted each other in silence. When Alfred stood with his weapon in readiness, Captain Crossby, who had kept his eyes fixed steadily on the man before him, said, warningly, "You remember!" and rejoined Alfred. Hiram watched them disappear in the fog. When they were out of sight, and as he turned towards his cabin, he seemed to be taken with passion. His face grew fiery red in a moment, the veins in his neck swelled, his eyes became redder with blood, and he rattled and knocked his teeth together, at the same time bursting out every few seconds in a short, guttural growl of a laugh: this throaty, hoarse sound, and the gnashing of his teeth, occurring at the same moment, sounded, a few feet away in the fog, as if a dog were worrying some animal, which in return was clapping its bloody teeth at him.

Alfred lived in his cabin alone, and salted down his venison and bear's-meat. He neither saw nor heard of Hiram or Lucinda.

There was a discussion of the affair at the mill. The general opinion was clearly that Mr. Bannerman should have removed Mr. Stott from the scene of his activities. If he had not, it was not their business. Mr. Brown was especially severe on Alfred. But the whole transaction seemed to him like some ghastly error in his accounts. There was something about it all that didn't add up—to him, so he averred.

It was reported later on that Lucinda took extraordinary pains with Hiram's " brats," but that she herself was careless and unkempt, and that she had lost her " countenance."

## V

It was a year after that when Hiram fell ill. Alfred first heard of it through Captain Crossby. The latter told him that Lucinda had walked all the way to the mill to ask her father for help, and that Amri had given her food for herself, as much as would do her two days, and a mule to carry her back to Hiram's, and had gone with her himself to within sight of the cabin ; but farther he wouldn't go and more food he wouldn't give ; and he had said very plainly at parting, he being always a plain speaker, that he would feed Lucinda and roof her and affectionate her if she took to livin' and keepin' house with a catamount—it wasn't wedbreach he minded, that was all in the way o' life ; but as for Hiram and hisn, he'd as soon feed a hole in hell as fill their empty stomachs. If they starved, it was God's own will, and a redemption at that.

With this sentiment every one at the mill agreed.

Alfred, as he returned from the mill the same day, wondered how Lucinda would make out to " do " for herself and the three children with Hiram ill. It was still warm weather; no doubt Hiram's cabin was well stocked.

About a week later Alfred had a restless night. The wind rose with the evening, and the sky foretold a heavy snow. Alfred dreamed confusedly, and woke repeatedly to hear the wind constantly increasing in violence. Towards dawn, in his dreams he saw Lucinda before him in deep snow, striving to lift some heavy object that lay before her, and which Alfred from his position could not see. He dreamed this picture twice. The third time he started up, for he seemed to hear his wife call, and saw her face with such distinctness that he was able to judge whether, as he had heard, she had " paled out." But in his dream she was rosier than ever. He made no effort to sleep again. However, as he sat alone before the fire, and listened to the wind roaring loudly outside, his thoughts came upon him troublous and thick. He felt beset with them and in danger from them. For this there was a remedy. He took his axe from the corner, drew on his coat, and went out. The wind came from the north with a steady rush, and the snow, slanting down to the earth in a whirling mist of fine, dry flakes, was scurried away as soon as it had fallen, and piled into drifts behind whatever obstruction happened to lie as a break to the wind.

In the thick of the storm, and half-blinded by the force with which the wind blew the fine flakes of snow against his eyes, Alfred set to work vigorously upon a tree at the edge of his clearing. After some hours of swinging his axe the day grayed faintly through the falling snow; and the dangerous flood of his thoughts having passed away with the night and labor, Alfred returned to his cabin.

When he had cooked and eaten he looked at the size and depth of the drifts outside, now first visible in the dawning light, and seemed suddenly to make up his mind.

In another hour's time he was striding through the woods, a pack of venison, bear's-meat, and corn-flour on his back.

He made his way down the ridge to the swamp where stood Hiram's cabin. As he came out of the thicket he saw that the cabin was half snowed under on the north side; at the south the ground was bare. He knocked. . There was no answer.

Again he knocked, and fancied he heard a groan. He entered cautiously, not without a fear of being shot in the back. The room was in the utmost disorder, and so hot from a fire of hickory logs that the panes were clouded. Hiram lay sprawling on the bed, under a dirty quilt of all the colors of the rainbow, groaning not much above a whisper.

"Hiram," said Alfred, softly.

The form of the sick man appeared to leap from his bed. He staggered among the bed-clothes and grasped for his rifle, which hung above his head along a rafter. Alfred instantly seized him by the shin, and the two men were rolling on the floor together as Lucinda entered and gave a cry of horror, supposing that she saw a murder.

"Speak to him; he isn't hurt," said Alfred, sitting on the sick man's chest. And Lucinda making no answer, he repeated, "Speak to him; make him keep quiet."

"I can't quiet him," cried Lucinda; "he's just crazy; he's not in his senses; he'll kill you if you let him up."

"Give me a rope," said Alfred; and with the rope thus obtained he bound the prostrate man and laid him on the bed.

As he turned to Lucinda he now saw her for the first time in a year. She was changed. For not only was she standing there nervously catching at her dress with her fingers, a look of pain and confusion on her face, but she was also haggard. The color still burned in her sunken cheeks, but it looked almost unnatural now, and seemed, as Alfred regarded her, to flicker and waver, like the flame and light of a candle which had burned below the socket, and might presently go out and leave her cold and wasted and as pale as wax forever after. There was about her expression, as she began to recover from her fright, something of a settled but none the less bitter self-contempt. The hair that she used to tie up with a ribbon was laced round now with a leather shoe-string, and looked knotted and tangled in its masses, while her dress was greasy and slovenly put on. She looked at Alfred as if she feared him.

"What are you come for?" she said, at length.

"I heard say he was sick and couldn't rightly do for you, and I judged that with last night's snow you'd be hurried some to do for yourself, and for him down, and his children; so I came to bring that."

Alfred pointed to the pack on the floor.

The girl made no answer. Then she broke out, suddenly, "You don't say you came to this house, and *me*, to bring food-stuff to *him?*"

"Seeing that he's sick," said Alfred, "I did. I bring you both, and the children, what 'll keep hunger from the door."

Lucinda's eyes—the feature of her face that had changed least—were so bright, with such a questioning brightness, as she gazed at Alfred, that she seemed to desire to throw light from them into his hidden soul. What he really meant, his way of feeling, was still dark to her; whether he was "a sheep," as Hiram had affirmed, a creature not to consider, without the natural passions of jealousy and anger, a coward, or whether there was something she had failed to get at behind that appearance of quiet, and the sad, innocent eyes that avoided hers

—as to all this she had remained uncertain. But this present action of his seemed to confirm her suspicions.

"You have forgiven him and me, then?" inquired she, the color blazing into her cheeks.

Alfred raised his eyes full upon her. He seemed to wonder what her thoughts were. At length he said, with great calm, and appearing to rest deliberately on those words which expressed most deeply his feeling and conviction:

"Lucinda, I have brought you and him food; and as long as that man there"—nodding to where the fevered man lay bound upon the bedstead, tossing his head from side to side, and groaning—"as long as that man there is down, I will give him and you the use o' my hands."

"You have forgiven me!" cried Lucinda, and she began to laugh in a wild, reckless way. Alfred raised one of his long arms with a motion of deprecation.

"Lucinda, you are woful mistaken. I have not forgiven you for your a-leaving me, and I never will. Let it, therefore, be no solace to you that I am able to forgive your offence, for able to do so I am not; no, nor willing; and I tell you, face to face, word for word, and p'intedly, what to your own heart is well known, that you broke my life, and made it a poor thing and hopeless, with your a-leaving me. Yes, you made my life such as my sleep is the dearest thing in it; and not to think of you, hit's the sweetest rest I can know. And though I bring you food-stuff, and though I will not stand by and see you to starve, nor his little ones, which are innocent, yet as I have a Maker, and as he looks on us two standing here, never will I forgive you for what you've undertook to do—never!"

The girl looked at him at first with a kind of contemptuous astonishment, then with considerable uncertainty as to his meaning. Finally she said, a little doubtfully, "I guess you're good—you're certainly good; but you ain't much of a man."

Alfred made no reply.

"You stayed away from me at the wrong time," continued Lucinda, with a sudden burst of emphasis. "Why in the world didn't you come home? It's all very well to be good. I'm not good. You were too easy and mild and soft, Alfred Bannerman; that's your life's trouble. Why didn't you take me and just give me one?"

Lucinda, with her figure drawn up and her fist closed to make it clear to Alfred what kind of "one" she had desired him to give her, looked for a moment more like her former self than he had hitherto seen her.

"Just give me one—hit me—when I got the mopes and miserables. Not you! You were too mild. I'll never forgive you that child's death—never!"

Alfred flushed, but made no reply; and the girl went on, with a short sob or two:

"Oh, it's just as well as it is. He's a

man; he knows his own mind," pointing to Hiram, who had grown quiet now. "He don't waste any mildness, I guess—not on me. But he's a man, anyhow, Alfred Bannerman, more'n God made you; and that's what's ruined me; and I wish—if it wasn't for the 'new one'—yes, I do! I do! I do!" —Lucinda broke into a passion of dry, angry sobs—"that I was dead and cold, and had no more to do with anything on this earth—nor anywhere!"

She turned her face from Alfred, and fell down on her knees, with her arms over something in the corner of the room, her body shaken and convulsed with a kind of wild grief.

"God have mercy on you," said Alfred—"on you and him and me!"

He heard a faint crying sound in the corner: it was the "new one" waking up. Alfred had not heard of the "new one" before, and now that he saw the cradle, with Lucinda still sobbing violently over it, and heard the voice of this child of his wife's, it seemed to him that something sacred had suddenly entered the house and made its presence felt. He looked at the man on the bed, and thought that perhaps now he would be true to Lucinda. He thought of his own dead child. The tears came suddenly into his eyes; he turned away, and went out of the cabin, and home.

He came every day after that, and did such work as Lucinda could ill do, chopping wood and the like; but he never spoke to her more than to bid her good-morning or good-night.

When Hiram began to recover, and saw Alfred working about the place, he asked himself if he, Hiram Stott, was a sane man. When he heard briefly, from Lucinda, why Alfred was there, he at once and finally concluded that Alfred was not a sane man.

## VI

As the spring drew on Hiram recovered
himself completely, and in June he took his
three older children over to their uncle's in
Case County. He made three trips, and
carried a good many of his more important
possessions with him. The last time he left
the mules there. Lucinda was surprised;
but she concluded that Hiram was tired of
the "old place," and was going to try Case
County. She was willing to do the same.
Her final conclusion about Alfred was that
he was "queer"—the only judgment possible, be it said, when comprehension of mo-
tive fails; and further, that he was "mild,"
and "no great of a man." She thought of
him often; and when she thought of their
first days together she was very apt to cry.
But that was all desperately over. If he
had only not been so "mild"! For Hiram
her feeling was simple: he was this, or that,

or what might be; but he was the father
of the "new one," and when she had the
"miserables" he gave her the mighty coun-
ter-irritant of blows. She never asked herself if she loved or had loved him; she
simply saw in him the person who was her
refuge from herself.

It was during the evening of a hot July
day, when Alfred, successful enough this
year in his farm work, was coming home
down the Highland Ridge from salting
cattle of his own, that he heard and then
saw a man in the distance making towards
him along the ridge. The man had a pack.
It was Hiram. He eyed Alfred suspiciously
as he passed, bending under his load, a rifle
in one hand and his hat in the other, with
which every now and then he wiped the
sweat from his forehead. Neither spoke.
But Hiram, once his back was presented to
Alfred, kept his neck crooked round over
his shoulder, looking after the other, who

was walking straight ahead with his gun and
an empty salt-bag in one hand. He had a
shrewd suspicion that Alfred might turn
suddenly and shoot. He even felt the spot
in his back where the ball would hit; and
fearing this, he stumbled heavily along, his
head twisted over his shoulder, until Alfred
was out of sight; then he hitched his pack
up on his back, wiped the sweat from his
face again with his hat, and made the sort
of worrying, chuckling, hoarse sounds that
were with him laughter and fullness of soul;
and so passed on his way, feeling more in-
finitely pleased with and proud of himself,
and more tickled by the smooth success of
his scheme, than ever before in his life since
the day he had shot Joe Rayner up an ash-
tree.

As Alfred came swinging up to his cabin
Captain Crossby was sitting on the step.
He looked grave.

"Have you heard the news of Hiram?"
said he, abruptly.

" I just passed him," observed Alfred.

" Where ?"

" On the Highland Ridge, going north."

" He has left Lucinda," said Captain Crossby.

" He has?" said Alfred.

" Has," replied his friend, briefly.

Alfred looked away across the wooded hills towards the sunset. His big eyes seemed suddenly as full of pity and distress as human eyes can be.

" Uncle Dan, I guess we must kill that man." Alfred spoke with his usual deliberation.

" Well, now, that's just my notion edzackly," returned the old man.

In a few minutes the two set out, taking ammunition and three days' rations. They kept together up the Highland Ridge, walking late into the night. The next morning they separated. Captain Crossby was to go along the ridge north, watching at daybreak and towards dark for Hiram's smoke. Alfred pursued the course of the Snake Branch. Hiram, whom they believed to be making for Case County, might have taken either trail. Towards evening of the second day Alfred saw broken twigs and footprints, and pressed on. It was afternoon of the following day, as he came cautiously around a turn in the little river, that he first saw the man he wished to kill. The Snake Branch was hemmed in by high mountains here, darkened on either side and overhung by tall pines and laurel; and thus darkened and overhung, it went noisily gushing down among stones and rocks. Alfred saw Hiram some few hundred paces away, jumping from stone to stone lightly under his heavy pack and making pretty fast time. In a few minutes he was near enough, unseen by Hiram, to have shot him in the back. Instead, he called out. The man ahead started, and, disengaging himself from his pack with very considerable celerity, dropped behind a rock in a foot or two

of water. Alfred was exposed, but he had
little fear that his opponent would risk his
single ball on him so long as he was in quick
motion, and accordingly he splashed through
the shallow water, and ran rapidly along the
beach, thus in a few moments making a flank
movement, and forcing the man behind the
rock to disclose himself, which he did immediately, standing up, taking quick aim,
and firing. The shot took effect. Alfred
stopped, shaken with the sudden blow of a
bullet scathing the flesh of his shoulder; but
as Hiram turned to make the opposite bank
he levelled his rifle in turn and fired. While
the narrow and rocky gorge was still full of
echoes he heard a heavy splash, and as the
smoke cleared away, floating down-stream,
he perceived the man lying in the water.
He loaded, and then crossed to the spot.
Hiram's rifle lay between the rocks, still
smoking; the pack was some feet away in
shallow water; and the man himself, as Alfred lugged him heavily out, was dead. He

laid the body on a rock, and, standing in the
water up to his knees, looked sadly at the
man that had been his enemy.

" My friend, it had to be."

He had never called him his friend before,
and why he did so now he would scarcely
have known had he thought of it.

" You made bad work when you were up
and doin', and now you're down and dead,
and it's a God blessing you are. I am sorry
for you."

He said this, shaking his head, with the
simplicity of grief, and as if indeed he re-
gretted something he had always expected
to regret.

" You're dead, and it's but right you should
be. Now that's the truth."

Alfred made a fire on the bank and cooked
his evening meal. As his own corn-meal
had given out he opened Hiram's pack, and
cooked and ate the dead man's. The dodger
thus made gave him no qualms. Nor did he
eat any the less that as he sat on the sand

he could look across to where the setting
sunlight fell on the face on the rock.  Every
now and then he shook his head and sighed,
but said nothing.

He buried Hiram's body in the woods
and returned home.

Uncle Dan turned up three days afterwards,
and went the next morning to the mill to tell
Amri Carr.

Alfred set out at the same time for Hiram's cabin.  He found Lucinda pale, slovenly, and red-eyed with weeping.  As he approached, she said, "Read that."  It was a
scrawl of charcoal on paper.

Before goin'.  Bein' sick of you, I have left and
gone.  Alfred he'll take you back.

HIRAM STOTT.

"I have made my mistake, and I must
bide by it," said Lucinda, in a shrill voice.
"Did you know this?"

"I did," replied Alfred.

"He told you?"  Lucinda laughed dryly.

"So you let him do what you said you would not let him do, eh? He always said you were a sheep, Alfred."

Alfred looked down at her pityingly.

"He's dead," he said, simply. "I shot him through the heart last Thursday, about sunset, in the Snake Branch. He had his chance, and put me one here" — pointing to his shoulder; "but he's dead now. I came to take you to your fawther."

Lucinda was completely overcome with astonishment. She felt, or pretended to feel, no grief for Hiram. But she was astonished to that degree that she said nothing.

They started for Carr's Mill the next day. Alfred had loaned his mule, and as Hiram had taken his away a month ago they were obliged to walk. Alfred carried the "new one" in its cradle on his shoulder. Lucinda came behind. As she saw Alfred walking along in front of her, the "new one" merrily gurgling at the tree-tops, clearly pleased with the mode of conveyance and the swaying and

easy motion of it, she felt less sick at heart,
less sore, than she had for months, but much
more confused. She could not understand
it. Alfred was so much smoke—a riddle to
her of the darkest kind. She trudged wearily behind, and wondered, and thought of
Hiram with pity, and hate, and almost love,
and a strong dread of his being near about
somewhere, and not dead at all. Amri
Carr came out and took Alfred by the
hand. He had heard it all from Uncle
Dan.

"Alfred Bannerman," said he, "hit's a redemption! I'll go down with you to Somer-
set to-morrow, and we'll fix the sheriff. Oh,
ho!"

Mr. Carr blew a mighty blast, as if in the
act of clearing away all obstructions of a
legal nature from his son-in-law's path; to
which, with a sort of shout, he added another,
as if he would blow some feeble posse, with
*habeas corpus* attached, like the tail to a kite,
into the remotest departments of the sky.

Her mother took Lucinda into the house
and kissed her.

"Kiss your sister," she said to the children.

They did so, and warmly enough ; but Lucinda was too tired to know or care.

"Let her learn by this," said Amri to his
wife, and indeed to Lucinda—"let her learn
by this that a hog ain't a man, and contrairy-
wise. 'Live and learn'—that's my motto.
Alfred says he won't take her back, mother ;
he says she's broken his heart. I kind o'
believe she has. 'Live and learn'—that's
what I say. She'll know better next time."


## VII

Alfred was home again in a day or two.
The life which he now took up was as soli-
tary as it could well be. He had plenty of
time, therefore, to think and recall. Lucinda
passed to and fro in his mind continually,
and he recalled Hiram, dead and alive, not

seldom. He would sit over his fire in the cabin, or over his camp-fire—for, now that he had no wife or child, he had taken up hunting again, and spent weeks alone in the Big Pines — and there recall his last encounter with Hiram: how he had looked at a distance, skipping from rock to rock; how he had appeared at the moment he himself had shot; how his face and wet hair looked after death.

He saw all these things clearly, and, being much alone, necessarily saw them often; but they affected him with no degree of remorse. He had even no regret for what he had done. It seemed to him only that he had accomplished a needful act — that he had removed a nuisance. It gave him satisfaction when he thought of it now, exactly as it had done when he stood over Hiram's body laid on the rock, and said it was right that he should be dead, and that was the truth.

Towards spring of that year it was rumored

that Hiram's uncle from Case County, with
his two grown-up sons, had been seen about.
They had been so prolific of protestations,
and so loud in these, against any one's supposing that they had come for retaliation,
that Captain Crossby, getting wind of them
and their words, rode directly up to inform
Alfred that they were probably bent on vengeance.  Alfred said he had no doubt that
with time they would think better of it ; and
presently the three disappeared from sight
of man or hearing.  They had descended
upon Hiram's cabin, and taken all that Amri
Carr had left there, which was not a great
deal.  The cabin was deserted now, and
Hiram's uncle and his two sons had not been
heard of for a fortnight, when one evening,
as Alfred was stroking a kitten which had
been left to starve and mew most piteously
about Hiram's deserted place, and which he
had accordingly claimed and taken home, he
heard a sharp rap on one of the oak slabs
that served for shingles on his cabin roof.  It

was followed by a report at no great distance. Alfred took down his rifle, and put a short knife in his belt. He sallied out, and when in a minute's time the same thing happened again, the flash of the rifle being apparent to him on the crest of the hill above, he promptly fired at this flash. His shot was answered by two in return. Then all was still, and there were no more shots fired that night. But about a week later, this time after midnight, two more balls came tapping upon his roof. As there was no third, Alfred could make no likely return ; but when, the very next night, the thing occurred again, and a ball crashed through the roof, sinking itself into the log opposite, Alfred determined that Hiram's uncle was trying to scare him into leaving his cabin temporarily, when he and his sons would doubtless gut and burn it in his absence. He made up his mind that he would disappoint them, and accordingly passed four nights in watch, forty paces, as near as he could judge,

from the spot whence the shots had been
fired on the hilltop.    The fifth night, towards
morning, he heard muffled voices, and presently saw the three figures plainly, but concluded not to shoot at once.   Two of the
figures, as he expected, levelled their rifles
and fired at the little cabin below.   Alfred
could have killed his man, but he felt, as
he said afterwards, that anybody who would
play such a trick must be a boy or foolish,
and he didn't like to chance killing a boy
or a fool.   He did fire, aiming, however, at
about the ankle of the dimly seen man.
There was a howl, and a sudden scuffling
flight. " Barked him," thought Alfred.  But
he was not content with so much, and began a vigorous pursuit, which lasted until
the evening of the day then about to dawn.
Twice during this day he sighted his three
men, and was twice fired upon, answering in
kind now, but at great distance, through a
drizzling rain and a tangle of underbrush.
As he was himself much exhausted at the

close of the day, and as he had found blood in the track of one of the three men, he concluded that he had given them enough to make it unlikely that they would worry him again. So he returned home, trying to think how many men his Case County marauders could have supposed were hot upon their pursuit.

When Alfred related this to Uncle Dan, the old man was perhaps as much amused as ever in his life. He met Mr. Carr in Mr. Brown's store a few days later, Lucinda and her mother both standing by, and seized the opportunity to repeat the entire tale, not without embellishment and an added member or so to the Case County crew.

"Alfred Bannerman's tasted blood," said he, dryly, "and hit's my notion he's goin' to be a terrible dangerous man—comes the time he get his full growth."

Captain Crossby threw his head back, looked out at old Carr, and laughed without a sound for about a minute. He knew very well that Lucinda had thought Alfred too mild, and the temptation of her presence was accordingly too great for him.

Mr. Carr heard the tale with a series of explosive breaths and exclamations.

"Well," he said, at the conclusion, realizing very clearly that the story was aimed at Lucinda, " people gets mistaken in people, and people ain't always what people thinks. Most men 'll fight and scratch — like Mr. Brown here — but Alfred he's a slaughterer ! Why, he's a danger to the peace! Chase a whole pack o' thieves and disturbers! Bark their shins! And shoot at 'em for thirty miles! In the night at that! And all the time to look as mild and gentle as a little ewe lamb!"

Mr. Carr burst into a roaring laugh, which shook him in all his limbs, as if he were a tree struck suddenly by a strong wind. He waved his arms, and ran his hands through his hair, apparently in the desire to get all

16

the relief he could. Captain Crossby responded silently.

"When Alfred bleats he signifies blood," said Mr. Carr, bringing both his fists down on the counter to give exit to some of the volume and violence of his mirth, and thereby causing Mr. Brown to start and emit a feeble exclamation.

Lucinda said nothing, but remembered the story, and took care to hear it repeated. At that time she was too worn, and too little herself, to see clearly; but later she began to feel that she had mistaken Alfred. That he was " mild," that he lacked some asperity of nature, some commanding, enforcing quality, at least towards her, was plain enough still; or, at all events, that, unlike the men she was accustomed to, he chose not to allow himself to be imperative with his wife, and gave her a freedom that Lucinda herself felt she was ill able to bear. All this was plain to her now. In her opinion, no man had any right to be as soft and yield-

ing as Alfred had been. She said to herself
that she hated him for it. But, on the other
hand, he was no coward; although why he
had not killed Hiram at once she felt would
be a riddle to her forever. But, for the rest,
Alfred seemed to be rather unusually ready
and successful with his rifle, and not to know
what fear was. She wished he had shown
her that side of his character—*in time.*

The following spring Alfred came down
to the mill to help Captain Crossby with his
harvesting, and remained there a month or
so. He passed Lucinda more than once,
but the girl, with her head carried very high
and her eyes in another direction, appeared
not to see him. She hated him to be anywhere near, and could have killed him whenever he passed her. Alfred never came to
Mr. Carr's cabin, but he gave the old man
six wild-cat skins for the "new one," all
sewed roughly together by himself.

The day before he left Captain Crossby's
he knocked at Mr. Carr's door. Lucinda

happened to be sitting on the floor inside, the rest of the household being absent. She was teaching the "new one" how to crawl. She said "Come in!" blithely enough; for hard work, the "new one's" pranks and growth, and the rough, busy, noisy, laughing, and joking household of people among whom she had lived had put the color in her cheeks again, and renewed her physically and morally in the good course of time.

"Come in!" she cried out.

But when she saw the visitor she started up from the floor, looking to Alfred just as she used to in the days when he first knew her—rosy and fresh and proud, except perhaps for something softer and kinder in the expression of her face.

She gazed at Alfred now without a word.

"If I may come in," said Alfred. He had a spray of blossoms in his hand, and tossed it to the "new one." "If I'm welcome," he said, tentatively, and without the usual assured quiet of his demeanor.

"You're not welcome," said Lucinda, abruptly. The color rose to her face. Alfred noticed, as she stood there, looking very angry and breathing fast, that her hair was tied with a blue ribbon again.

"That is," she added—"come in ; no one you want to see 's here—but you are welcome."

Alfred had suddenly lost the look of hope with which he had entered.

"I am certainly right sorry if I am much unwelcome."

He stood before her, with his long arms hanging down, and looking at her with the serious, innocent eyes that made her cry in her sleep, and wake crying when she saw him and them in a dream.

Lucinda felt anger, and pity for herself, and hate of Alfred, and despair, and some other feeling, vague and strong, left over from her former life—she hardly knew what to call it, or even what it was—all rising and swelling and coming heavily upon her, and carrying her off her feet, like a succession of waves: only to her they seemed to come from all quarters, and from underneath, and to clash and crash violently together. She stood, trying to control herself.

"Lucinda," said Alfred, evidently also trying to get the better of some emotion that appeared to catch him in the voice— "Lucinda, I want you to come and live with me again."

The girl's expression suddenly fell, the color left her cheeks, a look almost of fright and weakness overcame her, changing back again to life and boldness as suddenly.

"If you can care enough to make you want to do it," continued Alfred, speaking slowly. "I am very poor of a hand at forgiveness, and I wish not to make any make-believes of forgiving you; for what you did is done, and hit cost a life. But all I say now is, if you think you will be happier than in the old days—"

Lucinda clapped her hands together, and seemed almost to gasp for breath as she burst in: "Alfred Bannerman, unless you can care for me I won't go—not a step! I won't have your pity!"

"I give you none," said Alfred, bluntly.

"If you want me, knowing what I am, what I was, and having suffered from me—knowing as I am a bad girl, and was false to you, and a wicked devil—and if knowing all that, and those, you can care—why, then, I'll say too that I was terrible mistaken in you, and that you're the only man—right, true man—I ever met up to! And I ain't regrettin' nothing, and I won't make no promise—but—but—"

Lucinda tossed her head back as if the words stifled her. Her hair came down and fell over her shoulders in a mass, and the color flared into her face and down her neck.

"Lucy, I want you; will you come?" said Alfred.

He moved a step towards her. There was some word on her tongue, but what it was he never knew, for she seemed to struggle with it in a kind of death-agony of expression, the blood flushing her more and more, and her entire figure trembling, until Alfred took both her hands in his, when she burst into tears and sobs, and cried as if she never expected to have an opportunity of crying again.

"Lucy," said Alfred, "will you come and try?"—very much fearing that this explosion of grief in tears meant "No" to the new hope he had so slowly formed.

"'Ain't I said I would!" cried out Lucinda, indignantly, between her sobs.

Not many days after the "new one" was crawling about Alfred's cabin, mauling the kitten in a shocking and inhuman manner, and setting up unheard-of yells at the most distant approach of hunger.

"I couldn't live without him now," said Alfred; "and I do hate to see a little one grow up wanting its true fawther, without some kind of a makeshift."

Lucinda loved him dearly when he said that.

"I do hate it when one of these little ones dies," continued Alfred, thinking sadly of his own baby. "Hit don't seem right; they're born with such a heap o' trouble that it does seem they ought to live and be a happiness to themselves."

Almost every morning, dull or bright, of the spring and summer, if you had chanced to pass by at the foot of Alfred Bannerman's hill, you would have heard a girl's voice floating down from the cabin where she was at her work, where she had come to live again, happily this time, with "the only man — right, true man — she had ever met up to."

THE END

# THE WORKS OF
# WILLIAM DEAN HOWELLS

IMPRESSIONS AND EXPERIENCES. 12mo, Cloth, Uncut Edges and Gilt Top, $1 50.

MY LITERARY PASSIONS. 12mo, Cloth, $1 50.

STOPS OF VARIOUS QUILLS. Poems. Illustrated by HOWARD PYLE. 4to, Cloth, Ornamental, Uncut Edges and Gilt Top, $2 50.

THE DAY OF THEIR WEDDING. A Story. Illustrated by T. DE THULSTRUP. 12mo, Cloth, $1 25.

A TRAVELER FROM ALTRURIA. A Romance. 12mo, Cloth, $1 50; Paper, 50 cents.

THE COAST OF BOHEMIA. A Novel. Illustrated. 12mo, Cloth, $1 50.

THE WORLD OF CHANCE. A Novel. 12mo, Cloth, $1 50; Paper, 60 cents.

THE QUALITY OF MERCY. A Novel. 12mo, Cloth, $1 50; Paper, 75 cents.

AN IMPERATIVE DUTY. A Novel. 12mo, Cloth, $1 00; Paper, 50 cents.

A HAZARD OF NEW FORTUNES. A Novel. Two Volumes. 12mo, Cloth, $2 00; Illustrated, 12mo, Paper, $1 00.

A PARTING AND A MEETING. Illustrated. Square 32mo, Cloth, $1 00.

THE SHADOW OF A DREAM. A Story. 12mo, Cloth, $1 00; Paper, 50 cents.

ANNIE KILBURN. A Novel. 12mo, Cloth, $1 50; Paper, 75 cents.

APRIL HOPES. A Novel. 12mo, Cloth, $1 50; Paper, 75 cents.

CHRISTMAS EVERY DAY, AND OTHER STORIES. Illustrated. Post 8vo, Cloth, $1 25.

A BOY'S TOWN. Described for HARPER'S YOUNG PEOPLE. Illustrated. Post 8vo, Cloth, $1 25.

CRITICISM AND FICTION. With Portrait. 16mo, Cloth, $1 00. (In the Series "Harper's American Essayists.")

MODERN ITALIAN POETS. Essays and Versions. With Portraits. 12mo, Cloth, $2 00.

THE MOUSE-TRAP, AND OTHER FARCES. Illustrated. 12mo, Cloth, $1 00.

FARCES: A LIKELY STORY—THE MOUSE-TRAP—FIVE O'CLOCK TEA—EVENING DRESS—THE UNEXPECTED GUESTS—A LETTER OF INTRODUCTION — THE ALBANY DEPOT — THE GARROTERS. In Uniform Style: Illustrated. 32mo, Cloth, 50 cents each. ("Harper's Black and White Series.")

A LITTLE SWISS SOJOURN. Illustrated. 32mo, Cloth, 50 cents. ("Harper's Black and White Series.")

MY YEAR IN A LOG CABIN. Illustrated. 32mo, Cloth, 50 cents. ("Harper's Black and White Series.")

PUBLISHED BY HARPER & BROTHERS, NEW YORK.

*The above works are for sale by all booksellers, or will be mailed by the publishers, postage prepaid, on receipt of the price.*

www.ingramcontent.com/pod-product-compliance
Lightning Source LLC
Chambersburg PA
CBHW020513270326
41926CB00008B/859